STANDARD GRADE
MODERN STUDIES

Guch Dhillon, Joanne Kerr
and Wilma Simpson

Acknowledgements

The Publishers would like to thank the following for permission to reproduce copyright material:

Extracts from Question Papers are reprinted by permission of the Scottish Qualifications Authority.

Photo credits

Page 29 (top) © Scott Barbour/Getty Images, (bottom) © Bruno Vincent/Getty Images; Page 102 (top) UNICEF, (bottom) FAO.

Every effort has been made to trace all copyright holders, but if any have been inadvertently overlooked the Publishers will be pleased to make the necessary arrangements at the first opportunity.

Although every effort has been made to ensure that website addresses are correct at time of going to press, Hodder Gibson cannot be held responsible for the content of any website mentioned in this book. It is sometimes possible to find a relocated web page by typing in the address of the home page for a website in the URL window of your browser.

Hachette's policy is to use papers that are natural, renewable and recyclable products and made from wood grown in sustainable forests. The logging and manufacturing processes are expected to conform to the environmental regulations of the country of origin.

Orders: please contact Bookpoint Ltd, 130 Milton Park, Abingdon, Oxon OX14 4SB. Telephone: (44) 01235 827720. Fax: (44) 01235 400454. Lines are open 9.00–5.00, Monday to Saturday, with a 24-hour message answering service. Visit our website at www.hoddereducation.co.uk. Hodder Gibson can be contacted direct on: Tel: 0141 848 1609; Fax: 0141 889 6315; email: hoddergibson@hodder.co.uk

© Guch Dhillon, Joanne Kerr and Wilma Simpson 2006, 2009
First published in 2006 by
Hodder Gibson, an imprint of Hodder Education,
An Hachette UK Company,
2a Christie Street
Paisley PA1 1NB

This colour edition first published 2009

Impression number   5 4 3 2 1
Year   2012 2011 2010 2009

All rights reserved. Apart from any use permitted under UK copyright law, no part of this publication may be reproduced or transmitted in any form or by any means, electronic or mechanical, including photocopying and recording, or held within any information storage and retrieval system, without permission in writing from the publisher or under licence from the Copyright Licensing Agency Limited. Further details of such licences (for reprographic reproduction) may be obtained from the Copyright Licensing Agency Limited, Saffron House, 6–10 Kirby Street, London EC1N 8TS.

Cover photo © ImageState/Alamy
Illustrations by Richard Duszczak Cartoon Studio and Phoenix Photosetting
Typeset in 10.5 on 14pt Frutiger Light by Phoenix Photosetting, Chatham, Kent
Printed in Italy

A catalogue record for this title is available from the British Library

ISBN-13: 978 0340 973 974

CONTENTS

Introduction 1

Chapter 1   Syllabus Area 1 – Living in a Democracy 5
                  Politics
                  Pressure Groups
                  Trade Unions

Chapter 2   Syllabus Area 2 – Changing Society 42
                  The Elderly
                  The Unemployed
                  The Family

Chapter 3   Syllabus Area 3 – Ideologies 71
                  The USA

Chapter 4   Syllabus Area 4 – International Relations 87
                  Alliances
                  The Politics of Aid

Chapter 5   Enquiry Skills 110

INTRODUCTION

This book gives you summary notes of the Modern Studies Standard Grade course, information about revision techniques and detailed advice on how to answer questions. It will help you follow a study plan to achieve your best possible result in the Standard Grade Modern Studies examination.

Course Content

The Standard Grade Modern Studies course is divided into four units called **syllabus areas**. Each question in the examination paper covers one of these syllabus areas. For example:

Question 1: **Syllabus area 1 – Living in a Democracy**

Question 2: **Syllabus area 2 – Changing Society**

Question 3: **Syllabus area 3 – Ideologies**

Question 4: **Syllabus area 4 – International Relations**

Each syllabus area can be divided into topics. It is useful to remember the order in which the topics are likely to appear in the examination paper.

Question 1 Living in a Democracy	Question 2 Changing Society	Question 3 Ideologies	Question 4 International Relations
Politics	Elderly	(A) The USA*	Alliances
Pressure Groups	Unemployed	or	Politics of Aid
Trade Unions	Family	(B) China*	

* For Question 3 Ideologies answer **only** the questions on the topic you studied. Different schools will do different topics. In the course of this book we will focus on the more common of these, the USA.

The Concepts

The Modern Studies course is based on **concepts** (ideas) that explain how people behave in social and political situations. Every question in the examination refers to a concept.

Concept	Syllabus area
Representation Act, speak, or make decisions on behalf of other people, e.g. an MSP speaking for his/her constituents in the Scottish Parliament.	Living in a Democracy
Rights and responsibilities Freedoms we are entitled to and duties or obligations we have as a result, e.g. the right to vote and the responsibility to use the vote wisely.	Living in a Democracy and Ideologies (USA or China)
Participation Joining in, taking part, becoming involved, e.g. standing as a candidate in an election.	
Ideology Ideas and beliefs of a political or economic system, e.g. the USA is a capitalist democracy.	Changing Society and Ideologies (USA or China)
Equality Having the same level of wealth, status or well-being; usually looked at in terms of inequality, e.g. some elderly people have a lower living standard than others.	Changing Society and Ideologies (USA or China)
Need What individuals, groups or countries must have to survive and develop; usually looked at in terms of whether needs are being met, e.g. some developing countries find it difficult to meet their basic needs.	Changing Society and International Relations
Power Methods; alliances or countries have to defend their position and influence how others behave, e.g. countries join alliances in order to increase their power.	International Relations

Course Elements

Knowledge and Understanding (KU)

This accounts for **40%** of your final mark. KU questions usually start like this:

- ◆ **Describe**, meaning **tell me** what happens or what is done. For example, you could be asked to describe ways in which MPs represent the people in their constituency.

- **Give reasons**, meaning **why** something happens or is done. For example, you could be asked to give reasons why people should use their right to vote.
- **Explain**, meaning **how** and **why** something happens or is done. In other words, you have to describe **and** give reasons. For example, you could be asked to explain the advantages of the First Past the Post system. If you think about it, you can't really explain the advantages without describing what they are!

'Explain' questions are more complex and are therefore mainly used in the Credit examination.

Enquiry Skills (ES)

These account for **60%** of your final mark. This is **over half the marks**, so you need to know how to answer this type of question confidently. Most ES questions ask you to work with **sources** but you will also be asked about **investigating**.

Chapter 5 covers ES questions and how to answer them, but you can have a quick look now if you want find out about this before you start working through the book. Remember to return to that chapter in more detail later!

Revision Techniques

There are many revision techniques you could use when revising for your examination. They may include:

- testing by parents
- group work
- think–pair–share
- mnemonics
- memory maps/spider diagrams
- flash cards
- highlighted revision notes.

This is not an exhaustive list. There are many ways of revising. Don't be afraid to try a few methods. Don't worry if some of them don't suit you – not everyone works in the same way! With practice you'll find the method that works for you.

The Examination

After all the revising you'll be doing, you don't want to miss the examination!

Make sure you know:

- when you are sitting your examination (date and time)
- where you are sitting your examination (place and, if necessary, seat number).

Remember: most candidates sit **two** examination papers – either Foundation and General, or General and Credit. Make sure you know which examination papers you have to sit.

It is important to know how much time you have to answer the questions. It is also useful to know the time available for each syllabus area. For example:

Credit Paper	General Paper	Foundation Paper
2 hours	1 hour and 30 minutes	1 hour
30 minutes for each syllabus area	22 minutes for each syllabus area	15 minutes for each syllabus area

Remember

Use this table as a rough guide to allocating your time. One of the syllabus areas usually has questions that need more time because they are worth more marks or have longer source material. Make sure you give yourself enough time to answer these questions.

Above all, you **must** be fully prepared. This book can help you to prepare but you've also got to do your bit by studying hard. ***So don't delay, study today!***

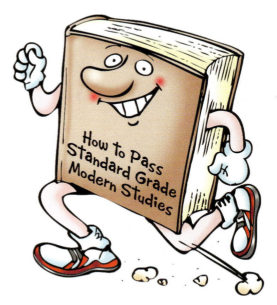

Figure 1 'Don't Delay, Study Today!'

Chapter 1

SYLLABUS AREA 1 – LIVING IN A DEMOCRACY

This syllabus area focuses on the concepts of **participation**, **representation**, and **rights and responsibilities**.

It can be divided into the topics of:

- Politics
- Pressure Groups
- Trade Unions.

You can revise the topics separately but the question in the examination may cover more than one topic.

Politics

Key Ideas

The UK is a democracy and people have the **right** to choose their **representatives** through regular elections with a choice of political parties and free media. However, people also have a **responsibility** to act within the law and to exercise their rights by **participating** in the political process.

What You Should Know

You could be asked questions about the following information in the examination:

- rights and responsibilities in a democracy
- right to vote
- representation
- electing an MP – First Past the Post system
- advantages and disadvantages of the First Past the Post system

What you should know continued ➢

Chapter 1

> ### What You Should Know continued
>
> - electing an MSP – Additional Member System
> - advantages and disadvantages of the Additional Member System
> - under-representation of women and ethnic minorities
> - how representatives help their constituents – MPs, MSPs and councillors
> - ways in which people can participate in politics.

Rights and responsibilities in a democracy

The UK is a **representative democracy**. This means representatives are elected (chosen) to speak for the views of the people they represent and make decisions on their behalf.

In a democracy, citizens have certain rights which are guaranteed, but with these come responsibilities (duties) to society.

Right to vote

British citizens (except the insane and long-term prisoners) have the **right** to vote if they are:

- over 18
- on the Electoral Register (list of voters).

But they also have a **responsibility** to:

- use their vote wisely e.g. find out about the candidates' policies before they vote
- accept the outcome of an election.

Right to stand as a candidate

Any British citizens over the age of 18 (except those who are disqualified, e.g. peers, people who are bankrupt, etc.) have the **right** to stand as a candidate if they are nominated by 10 electors and pay a deposit of £500 (which they lose if they get less than 5% of the votes). They do not have to be members of a political party but most are.

Candidates have a **responsibility** to campaign within the rules, e.g. they must appoint an election agent and spend only the allowed amount on election expenses (average of about £100,000 per UK constituency). They should also act honestly and legally if they are elected as a representative.

Right to protest

People have the **right** to form pressure groups and take part in meetings, demonstrations and other forms of campaigning in support of their cause.

Members of pressure groups have a **responsibility** to respect other people's opinions, to protest peacefully and not to damage people or property.

Right to a fair trial

If arrested, people have a **right** to be charged within 24 hours (this can be extended up to 4 days) and brought to trial within a certain amount of time. They have a right to present a defence and be represented by a lawyer. The Labour Government's plans to increase the time terror suspects could be detained without charge were defeated in Parliament.

People have a **responsibility** to obey the law, to serve on a jury if called and to tell the truth when giving evidence to the police or in a trial.

Freedom of speech

People have a **right** to criticise the government if they disagree with its policies or actions. For example, many people gathered together to criticise the government over the war in Iraq.

People have a **responsibility** not to slander (lie about) other people or to incite religious or racial hatred.

Freedom of the media

Newspapers, TV and radio have the **right** to criticise the government. Under the Freedom of Information Act the media have access to more information about the work of the government.

The media have a **responsibility** to report the facts accurately and fairly and not to libel (tell lies about) people or to incite hatred.

Why people should use their right to vote

In a democracy rights have corresponding responsibilities

Voting is a right or a freedom, so we have a responsibility, or moral duty, to use that right, especially since people like the Suffragettes fought in the past to gain the vote.

Some countries, like Australia and Belgium, think the responsibility to vote is so important that they make it compulsory and fine people who do not use their right to vote.

Voting gives you the right to a say in how you are governed

If people do not vote they have no say in how the country is governed. Voting lets representatives know the opinions of the people and the things that they want done.

Before the 2005 General Election the Liberal Democrats opposed the Labour Government policies on the war in Iraq and student tuition fees. Many people who were also against these policies voted for them and the Liberal Democrats won 12 seats from Labour.

Chapter 1

Low turnout is a threat to democracy

Voter apathy (people not bothering to vote) means that representatives are elected by only a few people but make important decisions for everyone. The turnout (number of people using their right to vote) has fallen in the last 50 years. In 1950, 84% voted in the General Election; in 2005 this had fallen to 61%. It is even lower for other elections: 51% (almost half) for the Scottish Parliament and local elections and only about a third for elections to the European Parliament.

A political party could come to power with a few votes and decide not to hold any more elections. The right to vote could be taken away or restricted and the country become a dictatorship. For example, there are still elections in the African country of Zimbabwe but opposition parties find it difficult to campaign and the President, Robert Mugabe, usually wins because he appoints enough members to parliament to give himself a majority.

Questions and Answers

The kind of questions you could be asked about rights and responsibilities are:

GENERAL

> *People should use their **right** to vote.*

Give **two** reasons why people should use their **right** to vote.

(Knowledge and Understanding, 4 marks)

CREDIT

> *The turnout at UK elections is seldom over 70%.*
> *People should use their vote.*

Why is it important that *people should use their vote*?

(Knowledge and Understanding, 4 marks)

Although both questions are worth **4** marks, you should notice some differences between the General and Credit questions.

General question	Credit question
Concept given in **bold** print	Concept not always given
Guidance on how much to write ('**two** reasons')	Guidance on how much to write *(4 marks)*
Straightforward statement	More complex statement
Descriptive answer ('*Give*')	Analytical answer ('*Why*')

Questions and *Answers* continued ➢

Chapter 1

Questions and Answers continued

Below is an example of how you would answer a General examination question using the Point, Explanation, Example method.

GENERAL

Point	The first reason why people should use their right to vote is because it is a freedom they have in a democracy like the UK.
Explanation	Rights usually have responsibilities attached so people have a duty or responsibility to protect democracy and prevent a dictatorship by using their vote.
Example	For example, if a lot of people do not vote, a political party could come to power with the support of a few people and decide to stay in power by restricting the right to vote like Robert Mugabe has done in Zimbabwe.

Don't worry if you can't think of an example – just try to expand your explanation. Below is an example of what the rest of your answer may look like as a flowing paragraph.

A second reason why people should vote is because they can choose MPs, MSPs and councillors who represent their opinions. This gives them a say in how the country is run and lets the government know that if they ignore public opinion they could be voted out of power. For example, in the 2005 General Election people who were against the war in Iraq made their opinion known by voting for parties like the Liberal Democrats who opposed the policy of the Labour Government.

The **Point**, **Explanation**, **Example** (**PEE**) layout may be familiar to you and is a useful way to lay out descriptive answers. For Credit answers add an L for Link, so the layout becomes **Point**, **Explanation**, **Example**, **Link** (**PEEL**).

Questions and Answers continued ➢

SYLLABUS AREA 1 – LIVING IN A DEMOCRACY

Chapter 1

Questions and Answers continued

CREDIT

Point	It is important that people should use their vote because a low turnout can be a threat to democracy.
Explanation	Democracy means that people have a say in how they are governed but when there is voter apathy and people do not bother to vote, a government can be elected by a few people but make important decisions for everyone.
Example	The number of people voting in the UK is falling. The turnout at the 2005 General Election was only 61%. Therefore, there is a possibility that the party in power might think the public are not interested. They might ignore public opinion and push through laws that are unpopular.
Link	People should use their vote to prevent this.

Think of your link as a way of proving that you have answered the question; try to show what your point proves and refer back to the question. You may also wish to mention the concept examined in the question. Don't panic – remember, we mentioned the concepts in the Introduction!

Below is an example of what the rest of your answer may look like as a flowing paragraph.

Voting is a right and like all rights it has a corresponding responsibility. The right to vote was hard won. People in the past, like the Suffragettes, fought and campaigned for democracy and the right of ordinary people to vote. Therefore people today have a duty to honour that by using their vote and not allowing it to be restricted or taken away. Some countries, like Australia, are so worried about falling turnout that they have made voting compulsory and fine people who do not use their vote. Therefore, there is a possibility that if people do not take their responsibility to vote seriously and only a few people vote, governments may think they do not need to hold regular elections. People should use their vote to protect it.

Representation

The UK is a representative democracy. This means representatives are elected (chosen) to speak for the views of the people they represent and make decisions on their behalf. In Scotland, people have the following elected representatives:

- Member of Parliament (MP) – House of Commons in London
- Member of the Scottish Parliament (MSP) – Scottish Parliament in Edinburgh
- Member of the European Parliament (MEP) – European Parliament in Strasbourg and Brussels
- Councillor – your local council chambers.

Candidates

Representatives start off as candidates. Candidates have to be over 18, be nominated by a number of electors in their area and pay a deposit (which they lose if they do not get enough votes). Although candidates can stand as independents (for example, Margo MacDonald is an independent MSP in the Scottish Parliament), most are selected by a political party. Each party has a different method of choosing candidates, but most allow local party members to participate in choosing the candidate for their area. Standing for a party gives a candidate a greater chance of success because the party funds (gives money for) the election campaign and the candidate may benefit from the national campaigning of the party. For example, some people vote for a particular party and are not too concerned about who the candidate is.

Political parties

Below is a memory map of the main political parties in Britain. Why not use the Internet to research political parties further? As you would expect, political leadership often changes. Make sure you are as up to date as possible.

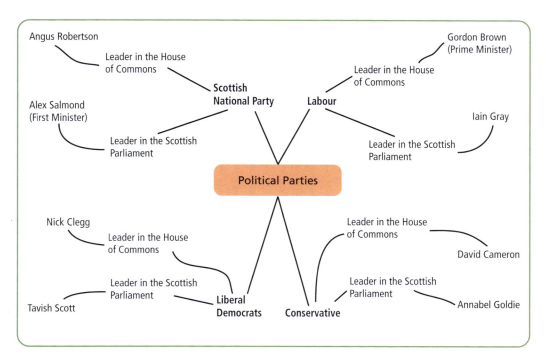

Figure 1.1 Political parties memory map

Chapter 1

Hints and Tips

Memory maps/spider diagrams are a useful way of summarising information. You can use the example on page 11 to help you build your own.

Electing an MP

The system used to elect MPs to the House of Commons is called **First Past the Post**. Every five years the UK holds a **General Election**. The Prime Minister can decide to hold a General Election in less than five years. For example, there were only four years between the General Election of 2001 and 2005. The UK is divided into 646 areas called constituencies and each constituency elects an MP. At the start of the General Election Parliament is dissolved (closed), candidates register and then start to campaign for votes.

646 constituencies = 646 seats = 646 MPs

Campaigning

In each constituency, candidates appoint an election agent and campaign for votes in various ways:

◆ **Distributing leaflets and posters**

 These give the name, party and main **policies** of the candidate. Policies are what the candidate intends to do if elected. All candidates can mail one leaflet to the voters in a constituency free of charge. Party workers also distribute leaflets door-to-door or in shopping centres, etc.

 People may agree with the policies, learn the name of the candidate and decide to vote for them.

◆ **Canvassing**

 Candidates, or volunteers, go door-to-door or tour shopping centres, community centres, etc. This allows people to meet the candidate, or a party member, and talk to him or her directly.

 People may like the candidate, have the opportunity to ask questions and agree with the candidate's views.

◆ **Loudspeaker cars and vans**

 Volunteers tour the constituency in the run-up to election day. They emphasise the name and party of the candidate and remind people to turn out to vote.

 People may decide to vote at the last minute. This reminds people of the name of the party and the candidate.

Chapter 1

Questions and Answers

GENERAL

> 'I would like to thank all our supporters for their help during the election campaign.'

Describe **two** ways in which supporters could help a political party during an election campaign.

(Knowledge and Understanding, 4 marks)

This question is about **participating** in electing a **representative** but you can use the information about campaigning in a constituency to help you to answer this question. You can use the **Point**, **Explain**, **Example** layout – that is, give the way a supporter can help, explain what it involves and illustrate it with an example.

Most candidates belong to a political party and the parties campaign nationally (over the whole country) in various ways.

- ### Publishing a manifesto
    A manifesto is a document giving details of the party's policies (what they intend to do if they win the election). Manifestos can be viewed and downloaded from the Internet. Details are also printed in newspapers, talked about in interviews and distributed in the form of leaflets and posters.

    Voters can compare party policies and may decide to vote for a party if they agree with its policies.

- ### Party political broadcasts
    The five 'terrestrial' TV channels broadcast party political broadcasts at peak viewing times. The more candidates a party has, the more broadcasts it gets.

    Parties make the programmes and decide on the content. Parties can put their policies across to lots of people.

- ### Media coverage
    The election is reported on TV and in newspapers:
    - TV has to be neutral – it cannot give one party more coverage than another. Elections are reported on the news, in current affairs programmes (e.g. *Panorama*), debates (e.g. *Election Specials*), etc.
    - Newspapers can be biased – they can show support for just one party. Sometimes newspapers change their support, e.g. *The Sun* changed from

SYLLABUS AREA 1 – LIVING IN A DEMOCRACY

Chapter 1

Conservative to Labour during the 1997 General Election campaign. *The Sun* gave itself credit for Labour's victory.

The increasing media coverage has led to accusations of General Elections becoming more about personalities than policies, with people being more interested in how the party leader comes across than in the policies he or she will introduce.

Election results: 'and the winner is ...'

Under the First Past the Post system, the candidate with **most votes** wins in a constituency and the party with **most seats (MPs)** in the House of Commons forms the government.

Hints and Tips

You might be given examples of election results in Enquiry Skills questions and asked to draw conclusions from them. It is important that you know how results are likely to be displayed.

It is also important to know what the results show.

*First look at **headings**: title, column or axis headings. For example, from the headings in Figure 1.2 you know that the information is about candidates and votes in Edinburgh South Constituency for the General Election in 2005.*

*Then look at the **information** given under each heading. For example, Neil Griffiths of the Labour Party won the Edinburgh South Constituency in 2005.*

*Check to see what **number** is being used – thousands, millions, percentages, pounds, etc. – and make sure you use the correct number in your answer. For example, turnout in Edinburgh South in the 2005 General Election was 69.4%.*

HINT!
Headings
Information
Number
Trend!

Hints and Tips continued ➤

Hints and Tips continued

*Finally, check the **trend**, i.e. any change over time. For example, if you were also given the Edinburgh South result for the 2001 General Election you would be able to see if the same party won both times, if the turnout had increased or decreased, etc.*

*Remember **HINT** – headings, information, number and trend – every time you use tables, graphs or charts.*

Constituency results

Winner is the candidate with most votes. Compare the number of votes with turnout and electorate to show that less than half the electorate voted for the winner.

Majority is the difference between 1st and 2nd, i.e. 14,188 – 13,783 = 405. A very small majority means it is a **marginal constituency** and any of the top three parties could win it next time.

UK General Election 2005 – Edinburgh South constituency

Candidate	Votes
Nigel Griffiths (Labour)	14,188
Marilyne MacLaren (Liberal Democrat)	13,783
Gavin Brown (Conservative)	10,291
Graham Sutµherland (SNP)	2,635
Steve Burgess (Scottish Green Party)	1,387
Morag Robertson (Scottish Socialist Party)	414
Majority	405
Turnout	42,698
% turnout	69.4%
Electorate	61,524

Turnout is the number of people who voted, usually shown as a percentage (%). Nearly one-third did not vote. Turnout is used to show the level of **participation** in the election, i.e. to show how many people took part.

Electorate is the number of people on the Electoral Register, i.e. the number of people who could have voted. It is useful to compare with the turnout to show how many people did not vote.

Figure 1.2

Chapter 1

National results

Winner is the party with most seats. 1 seat = 1 MP, so the winning party has the most MPs. They form the Government because they have enough support in the House of Commons to get their decisions made into laws. The leader of the winning party becomes **Prime Minister** and chooses a **Cabinet** of Ministers (Secretaries) to run Government Departments and help make decisions.

Winner (Labour) only got about one-third of the votes but over half the seats in the House of Commons. This is useful as an example of the **disadvantages** of First Past the Post i.e. the government is often elected with less than half the votes and is often **over-represented**, i.e. has more seats than votes.

UK General Election 2005

Party	Seats	% votes	% seats
Labour	356	35.3	55.1
Conservative	198	32.3	30.7
Liberal Democrat	62	22.1	9.6
SNP	6	1.5	0.9
Others	24	8.8	3.7
Total	646	100	100

Labour majority	66
Turnout	*61.2%*

Turnout is the percentage of the total electorate who voted. It is useful for showing level of participation in elections. You can combine it with percentage of votes to show how representative the government is, i.e. a low turnout combined with a small percentage of votes cast means the government was elected by a very small percentage of the total electorate.

Majority is the difference between the winner and **all** the other parties combined, i.e. 356–290 = 66. A large majority means the government can get laws through the House of Commons. A small majority means problems and the possibility of government defeats. One of the **advantages** of the First Past the Post system is that it usually gives a clear winner with a majority.

Smaller parties get a lot of votes but few seats. This is another example of the **disadvantages** of First Past the Post, i.e. smaller parties are often under-represented.

Figure 1.3

Advantages and disadvantages of the First Past the Post system

Advantages	Disadvantages
Easy to understand Voters simply put an X next to the candidate they want to vote for and the candidate with most votes (Xs) wins. **Quick result** Result is known the next day and there is no delay in forming a new government. **Clear winner** There is usually a clear winner with a majority in the House of Commons. This means strong government with enough MPs to get policies through Parliament. **Direct link between elected representative and constituents** You know who represents you and how to contact them.	**Wishes of voters not fully represented** In most constituencies the winner gets less than half the total votes. The party forming the government usually gets less than half the total votes in the country. **Parties not fairly represented** Smaller parties, like the Liberal Democrats, get a lot of votes but few seats (percentage of votes greater than percentage of seats). Larger parties like Labour get a bigger percentage of seats than votes (percentage of votes less than percentage of seats).

Hints and Tips

You can use information from the constituency and national results to give examples of the advantages and disadvantages of FPTP.

Electing an MSP

An MSP is a **Member of the Scottish Parliament**. The **Scottish Parliament** was set up in 1999 after a 'Yes' vote in a **referendum** (a vote by the whole electorate on whether to accept or reject a proposal). Certain parts of the government, like health, education, transport, justice and local government, are now **devolved**, and the Scottish Parliament deals with them without referring to the UK Parliament at Westminster. Other matters, like defence, foreign affairs, immigration (asylum), social security (benefits) and most taxation, are **reserved**, which means they are dealt with by the UK Parliament.

The **129** MSPs are elected by the **Additional Member System (AMS)**. This is a **proportional representation (PR)** system, which means there is a clear link between the number of votes a party receives and the number of seats it gets. The simplest PR system is called the **Party List**. Parties draw up a list of candidates and people vote for a party, not a candidate. The total votes for each party is converted to a percentage and this is used to decide how many of the party list are elected, e.g. if a party gets 40% of the votes, the first 40% of names on their list are elected.

The **Additional Member System** combines **First Past the Post** with the **Party List system**. It is a way of keeping the link between constituency and representative while giving smaller parties a fairer distribution of seats. This is important in Scotland where the Labour Party had more support than the other parties and was likely to always form the Scottish Government. Although good for the Labour Party, it was thought this might not be good for democracy. Labour would have no strong opposition in the Scottish Parliament and, if no other party had a chance of forming the Scottish Government, their supporters might feel their vote was 'wasted'.

1st part of BALLOT PAPER
Any Scottish Region

Conservative Party	X
Green Party	
Labour Party	
Scottish National Party	
Scottish Socialist Party	
Independent Candidates	

Regions: Highlands & Islands, Glasgow, North East Scotland, Mid Scotland & Fife, Lothians, South of Scotland, Central Scotland

2nd part of BALLOT PAPER
Any Scottish Constituency

W Brown (Labour)	X
A Jones (Liberal Democrat)	
K MacDonald (Scottish Nationalist)	
R Thomas (Conservative)	

On the first part of the ballot paper, voters choose a party. Additional MSPs for their region are chosen from party regional lists of candidates. The number of list MSPs each party gets depends on how many votes they get on the first part of the ballot paper and how many constituencies they win.

On the second part of the ballot paper voters choose their constituency MSP. The candidate with most votes is elected.

Figure 1.4 The Additional Member System (AMS)

Chapter 1

 You might be given examples of Scottish Parliament election results in Enquiry Skills questions and asked to draw conclusions from them. It is important that you know how results are likely to be displayed and what they show. These examples will help you to understand this.

Scottish Parliament election results 2007

The percentage of seats and votes are closely linked. List system means parties that win a lot of constituencies get fewer Regional List MSPs. Parties that win few constituencies 'top up' with Regional List MSPs.

Party	Constituency MSPs	Regional List MSPs	Total MSPs	% votes*	% seats
SNP	21	26	47	31.9	36.4
Labour	37	9	46	30.7	35.6
Conservative	4	13	17	15.2	13.2
Liberal Democrat	11	5	16	13.7	12.4
Green	0	2	2	2.1	1.6
Independent	0	1	1	1.1	0.8
Others	0	0	0	5.3	0.0
Total	73	56	129	100	100
Turnout	**52%**				

* Average of the percentage of constituency votes and regional list votes for each party

Smaller parties and independents stand and have a **better chance of being elected.**

No clear winner. SNP got most seats but did not have an overall majority, e.g. SNP 47 MSPs, all the rest 82 MSPs. Unlike the last two Scottish Parliament elections which resulted in a **coalition** between Labour and the Liberal Democrats with both parties providing members of the Scottish Government, the 2007 election resulted in a **minority SNP Scottish Government**. This means the SNP has to rely on the votes of MSPs from other parties to get its policies through the Scottish Parliament.

Figure 1.5 Scottish Parliament election results 2007

SYLLABUS AREA 1 – LIVING IN A DEMOCRACY

Advantages and disadvantages of AMS

Advantages	Disadvantages
Fairer result because the seats gained are more in line with the percentage of votes cast. This better reflects the wishes of Scottish voters.	Difficult to understand. For example, some voters are not sure how to complete the ballot paper. They think they have to vote for the same party.
Women and ethnic minorities are more likely to be elected because the parties put forward their list of candidates in order of preference.	The List vote puts too much power in the hands of political parties. It is the party, not the voter, that chooses which candidate to put at the top of the Regional List.
Voters have more choice because smaller parties put up more candidates. Voters can also choose independents or single issue groups.	Minority or coalition governments are likely because it is difficult for any single party to win over 50% of the seats. This makes it hard to pass laws.
Keeps link between MSP and constituents while giving a more representative distribution of seats in the Scottish Parliament.	Confusion between the role of Constituency and Regional List MSPs. For example, constituent might not know which MSP to approach for help.

Hints and Tips

Some people get confused about the difference between First Past the Post and AMS (a form of proportional representation, or PR). The main difference is what each system considers to be good representation.

For First Past the Post, good representation is a close link between constituency and representative, and a clear winning party able to deliver policies on behalf of its supporters.

For PR, good representation is a close link between number of votes and number of representatives, so that there are more parties in parliament and a wider representation of political views.

Under-representation

This refers to the fact that there are fewer women and ethnic minority representatives in proportion to the percentage of the population they make up.

Women	Ethnic minorities
1. Political parties might not select female candidates. For example, over three-quarters of the candidates in the 2005 General Election were male.	Political parties might not select ethnic minority candidates. For example, only 3% of the candidates in the 2005 General Election were from an ethnic minority.
2. Sexism may be present; voters may not vote for a female candidate. For example, only 18.9% of MPs in House of Commons are female.	Racism may be present; voters may not vote for an ethnic minority candidate. For example, only 2.3% of MPs (15) are from an ethnic minority.
3. The aggressive male atmosphere of the House of Commons puts some women off. They may find other areas of politics to work in that are more welcoming.	Language barriers; some older members of ethnic minorities do not speak fluent English. This can also reduce the number of ethnic minorities who vote.
4. Family reasons such as: ◆ working in London, but family based in constituency ◆ difficult hours of work; lots of evening work.	Few role models; few people to look up to, and aspire to, in politics, e.g. there are no ethnic minority MSPs following the death of Bashir Ahmad MSP.
But Scottish Parliament: ◆ has fixed working hours (roughly 9 to 5); breaks similar to school holidays; creche ◆ is relatively easy to get to in centre of Edinburgh ◆ uses PR. As a result, there are 44 female MSPs (34%); several are high ranking, e.g. Deputy First Minister, Nicola Sturgeon, and Conservative leader, Annabel Goldie.	**But** ◆ Labour and Conservative parties both have ethnic minority MPs. ◆ High-ranking ethnic minority politicians, e.g. Lady Scotland of Asthal was appointed Attorney General by Gordon Brown in June 2007. ◆ Operation Black Vote have an MP shadowing scheme to help ethnic minorities interested in being candidates.

Questions and Answers

CREDIT

'Elections to the UK parliament at Westminster use the *First Past the Post system.* Elections to the Scottish Parliament use the *Additional Member System.*'

Questions and Answers continued ➢

Chapter 1

Questions and Answers continued

Choose **either** the *First Past the Post system* **or** the *Additional Member System*. Explain the **advantages** of the system you have chosen.

(Knowledge and Understanding, 6 marks)

It is important to show that you understand the concept when you answer a question. You will notice that in this question the concept word does not appear. This often happens in the Credit examination and you have to figure out the concept for yourself. In this case, it is **representation** because the question is about the advantages of a method of electing representatives. Make sure you show clearly that you understand how the method you choose shows good representation of voters and/or parties.

You also have to make a choice, so choose the method of election for which you can give the most advantages. Remember: you have to *explain*, so give examples and say why you have included them and what they show. The election results you have just looked at should help you with this.

The question is worth 6 marks, so try to give two or three advantages, each with a point, explanation, example and link (**PEEL**). For example, if you chose First Past the Post you could start your answer like this:

Point	An advantage of the First Past the Post system is that it provides strong government because it usually results in a clear winner that is able to represent the views of its supporters.
Explanation	It is strong government because the winning party, who provide the Government, usually have an overall majority in the House of Commons. They do not have to rely on a coalition with another party. Coalitions can be weaker because they can break down.

Questions and *Answers* continued ➤

Questions and Answers continued

Example For example, in the 2005 General Election, the Labour Party won with an overall majority of 66 seats. Therefore they had the advantage of having enough MPs to get Labour policies through the House of Commons without relying on the votes of other parties. They can represent the views of Labour voters because they do not have to compromise their views to get the support of other parties.

Link First Past the Post is therefore a stable electoral system that almost always guarantees a clear winning result.

The other points that could be used to answer this question are:

◆ direct link between constituents and representative
◆ simple, quick and easy to understand the system of election.

Think about where you can find explanations and examples to expand these. For example, you could use how an MP represents constituents as an example of the first point, and how the First Past the Post system is organised for the second point. Remember: you can use examples from different parts of the topic and from your general knowledge, as long as you can link them back to the question!

How representatives help their constituents

How an MP or MSP represents constituents

1 In a constituency

Constituents can contact their representative by phone, letter or email, or attend the MP or MSP's **surgery**.

Surgeries are held at regular, advertised times in local halls, schools, community centres, etc. Constituents can talk to their representative in person and ask for help with problems. Constituents raise personal matters, like problems with housing, benefits, etc. and community matters, like local facilities being closed, problems with roads and traffic, etc.

What the MP or MSP can do

The MP or MSP can contact the Government Department, Agency or local council to enquire about the problem. Sometimes, when departments know the local MP or MSP is involved, they find an answer to the problem!

Chapter 1

The MP or MSP can also contact the local media (newspapers, radio and TV) to draw attention to the problem. Sometimes, the publicity will result in a quick solution to the problem!

Sometimes, the problem cannot be solved at a local level and the MP or MSP will raise the matter in parliament.

2 In the House of Commons or the Scottish Parliament

Method	How it can help
Question Time Asking a question to be answered by government leaders. *House of Commons (MPs)* MPs can use **Prime Minister's Question Time** to table a question for Gordon Brown. *Scottish Parliament (MSPs)* MSPs can use **First Minister's Questions** to table a question for Alex Salmond.	Government leaders do not like to admit in public that there is a problem. Often just tabling (submitting) a question will get it solved. The Prime Minister, or First Minster, can then announce the 'good news' or ask the MP, or MSP, to withdraw the question. If this does not happen, the extra publicity might get more representatives, and the media, involved in **lobbying** (persuading) Ministers to find a solution.
Debates Raising the matter in debates in the House of Commons (MPs) or the Scottish Parliament (MSPs).	Ministers have to defend the Government in debates. They do not like to hear about problems. To avoid bad publicity, they are likely to try to fix the problem before the next debate.
Voting The Government needs the support of MPs to get its policies made into laws. The Scottish Government also needs the support of MSPs for the same reason. A vote in the House of Commons is called a **division**. MPs are counted as they walk through the 'Aye' (Yes) or 'No' lobby (corridor) on either side of the Commons chamber. In the Scottish Parliament, MSPs vote by electronic keypad. In both cases, party **whips** (MPs or MSPs appointed by the party leader) try to make sure representatives stay loyal to their party.	MPs, or MSPs, have a chance to scrutinise (look carefully at) bills in committees. They can make sure they are what their constituents want and, if not, can suggest amendments (changes) to the bill. MPs, or MSPs, can speak in the debates on bills and try to persuade other representatives to vote their way. They might even get enough MPs, or MSPs, to vote against the bill and defeat the Government or Scottish Government.

Chapter 1

How a local councillor represents constituents

Meetings – councillors attend committee meetings or full council meetings to discuss, and make decisions about, local issues. For example, a councillor might attend the Education Committee and raise the concerns of the constituents in his/her ward about a proposed school closure.

Surgery – councillors hold surgeries which constituents can attend and ask for help with issues they are concerned about. The councillor may then raise the matter with the full council or a department.

Constituents can sometimes raise matters that are dealt with by central government and a councillor may contact the local MSP, MP or government department to help with the matter.

A councillor may use the local media to get publicity and local support for an issue they feel has not been dealt with.

Questions and Answers

GENERAL

> MSPs work on behalf of the people they represent.

Describe **one** way in which MSPs find out about problems in their local area.

AND

Describe **one** thing the MSP could do to draw attention to problems in his/her local area.

(Knowledge and Understanding, 4 marks)

This is an example of a question where the wording may not fit your notes exactly. Your notes may not have a heading that says 'how MSPs find out about problems in their local area', but you are likely to have information about how MSPs represent their constituents. If you think about it, MSPs can't represent constituents unless they know about their problems and attention is drawn to the problem when the MSP does something about it – so you do have the information to answer the question!

You can use the Point, Explain, Example (**PEE**) layout. For example, you might choose MSP's surgery as a way of finding out the problem faced by constituents. You might choose First Minister's Questions as a way of drawing attention to these problems. The concept is **representation**, so remember to use that word, or 'represent', 'represented', 'representing', etc. in your answer.

Questions and Answers continued ➤

Questions and Answers continued

Good examples count, so if you haven't already done so, start collecting up-to-date examples now. How? Well, you could look at your local newspaper and make a note of any current issues or problems that your MSP might have to deal with. Your MSP might even have a column in the local paper which mentions problems he or she has dealt with. You could check out the Scottish Parliament website at: www.scottish.parliament.uk. It has information about MSPs – you can look up your local MSP and find out the time and place of their surgery and lots of other things. There is also information about how the Scottish Parliament operates, including Question Time and the importance of committees within the Scottish Parliament.

CREDIT

> *Our elected representatives work on behalf of people in many different ways.*

Choose **either** local councillors **or** MSPs **or** MPs.

Describe, **in detail**, the ways in which the type of representative you have chosen works on behalf of the people they represent.

(Knowledge and Understanding, 6 marks)

To answer this question fully you must make sure that you make **two** or **three points** and **explain** them fully, giving **examples** and linking them back to the question.

Below is a list of points you may want to include in your answer:

◆ Question Time
◆ Voting
◆ Debates.

Remember: it is not enough to write a list, you must write *in detail*!

Chapter 1

Participation

People can **participate** (take part) in politics in a number of different ways. For example:

People can participate by ...	This is participation because ...
Voting in elections	People take part in electing their representatives like councillors, MPs, MSPs, etc.
Joining a political party	People join together to put forward their ideas for running the country. They can also take part in selecting party candidates.
Standing as a candidate	People take part in the elections to choose representatives for the local council, Scottish Parliament or House of Commons.
Campaigning in an election	People put forward the views of their political party and help to get their candidate elected.
Contacting their representatives by telephone, letter and email, or attending their surgery	People are taking part by making their views known to their councillor, MP or MSP.
Petitioning the Scottish Parliament	People can contact the Scottish Parliament and ask them to consider, and take action on, an issue.
Joining and campaigning with a pressure group	People are supporting a cause and trying to get representatives to take action.

SYLLABUS AREA 1 – LIVING IN A DEMOCRACY

Hints and Tips

You have come to the end of a section of work and you have a lot of information to remember. This is the time to think about how to organise your notes so that you are well prepared to answer the questions in the examination.

Choose a way to organise your notes to suit the way your mind works. For example, are you a list person, or a diagram person?

Try to organise the section you have just finished. Don't worry if you're not sure which method works for you. Pick the one that seems best at the moment. With practice, it will probably become your method – if not, there are plenty more, or you may even invent one of your own.

Chapter 1

Pressure Groups

Key Ideas

People have a **right** to join a pressure group and **participate** in activities to make their views known to **representatives**. Pressure groups, and their members, have a **responsibility** to campaign peacefully within the law.

What You Should Know

You could be asked questions about the following information in the examination:

- rights and responsibilities of pressure groups
- reasons why people join pressure groups
- ways in which pressure groups campaign.

What is a pressure group?

Pressure groups are organisations that believe in the same issue or cause. They want to influence decision makers (e.g. the Government) and get them to take action. They do not want to become the Government or even representatives. However, sometimes pressure groups have put up candidates to gain publicity for their cause and, on occasion, one of these candidates has been elected. For example, Jean Turner stood as a candidate for the Save Stobhill Hospital Campaign in the 2003 elections to the Scottish Parliament and was elected.

Rights and responsibilities of pressure groups

1. Pressure groups have the **right** to **criticise** (i.e. comment negatively on) the activities of the Government and other organisations.

    But they also have the **responsibility not to tell lies**.

    Misrepresenting (not telling the truth about) their cause can damage a pressure group. For example, when Shell wanted to dump its disused Brent Spar oil platform in the North Sea, Greenpeace damaged its own campaign when it gave incorrect figures for the amount of pollution this would cause.

2. Pressure groups have the **right** to **hold meetings and events** where people with similar beliefs can meet and discuss issues or show their support for a cause.

    But **meetings and events should be peaceful** and be about sharing information, not attacking people or property. For example, before the G8 Summit at Gleneagles in 2005, the Make Poverty History Campaign held a march in Edinburgh and Live 8 Concerts which were broadcast live and gained worldwide publicity.

Figure 1.6 Make Poverty History march in Edinburgh before the G8 Summit at Gleneagles, 2005

However, despite the pleas of the organisers, some of the demonstrators were not peaceful and this gave a bad image in the media.

Figure 1.7 Street protests in Edinburgh during the G8 Summit, 2005

3. Pressure groups have the **right** to **protest and demonstrate** to get their voices heard.

   But **protestors should obey the law**.

   Fathers 4 Justice did not always do this. For example, one of their members dressed as Batman and climbed onto a balcony of Buckingham Palace as a publicity stunt to draw attention to his cause.

4. Pressure groups have the **right** to **use the media** (local/national press, TV and radio) to publicise their cause.

   But they also have a responsibility to **give accurate information** or their cause may be damaged.

Why join a pressure group?

- You can create lots of publicity for your cause. For example, you can get on TV like Fathers 4 Justice who campaigned for the rights of fathers to gain access to, or custody of, their children.
- More people means more can be achieved – you've got more muscle like Greenpeace which is an international pressure group that campaigns to prevent pollution and protect the environment.
- Expert knowledge can be shared with the Government. For example, Age Concern campaigns on behalf of the elderly and contributes research, statistics and opinion to government committees on pensions and the elderly.
- You can gain professional and personal benefits. For example, trade unions are also pressure groups which campaign for better wages and conditions for their members.
- More members generally means a pressure group has more chance of success. It can organise and finance a professional campaign to 'drum-up' support. However, even relatively small groups can be successful if their cause is in line with the thoughts of the Government. For example, the Snowdrop Campaign, formed after the shootings at Dunblane Primary School, helped to persuade the Government to ban hand guns in the UK.

Hints and Tips

*You may be asked about pressure group **responsibilities** in particular. Remember that pressure groups have a responsibility to be **accurate** when using information and representing members' views. If they are not, membership may fall because people feel let down. The pressure group is unlikely to have its views taken seriously and could be prosecuted for making false claims. People have to be protected as well as represented so pressure groups have a responsibility to **keep within the law**, including informing police before a demonstration. A pressure group whose protests result in disruption and chaos may lose respect and membership.*

How pressure groups campaign

Method	Why it is a good way of influencing the Government?
Letter Campaign Letters are sent to the press, local councils, MPs/MSPs and officials asking for support, or protesting about an action already taken.	If enough letters are sent, representatives may realise the strength of the support and think they risk losing votes unless they take some action. For example, the Make Poverty History Campaign organised for letters and postcards to Tony Blair before the G8 Summit.
Petitions These are a collection of signatures of people who feel strongly about an issue and who want action. Groups can also petition the Scottish Parliament to take action on an issue through the Public Petitions Committee.	Shows how many people support the pressure group. This may persuade representatives that they risk losing votes unless they take action. For example, the Snowdrop Campaign's petition successfully persuaded the Government to ban hand guns.
Demonstrations People who feel strongly about an issue gather together to publicise their cause and persuade others to join. Supporters can carry banners and shout slogans to publicise their cause.	Large demonstrations attract publicity and show the strength of support for a pressure group. A large amount of support may persuade representatives to take action. For example, the Stop the War Coalition marches against the war in Iraq were some of the largest ever seen in the UK.
Involving the Media Newspapers and TV are used to get publicity and attract more people to the campaign. For example, Fathers 4 Justice staged stunts like dressing up as Batman and climbing onto Buckingham Palace to attract media attention. Media can also be used to educate the public about the issues involved. Representatives of pressure groups are often invited to take part in documentaries or studio debates. Most pressure groups have a website and produce free information leaflets, etc.	Media usually contact representatives of organisations or the Government for their reaction to and comments on pressure group claims. This can sometimes force the representatives to take action. The attention and publicity given by the media may increase support for, and membership of, the pressure group. For example, the celebrity support of Bob Geldof, Bono and Live 8, gave the Make Poverty History Campaign worldwide media attention.

Chapter 1

SYLLABUS AREA 1 – LIVING IN A DEMOCRACY

Questions and Answers

GENERAL

Describe, in detail, **two** methods used by pressure groups to influence the Government.

(Knowledge and Understanding, 4 marks)

To answer this question fully you must make sure that you make **two points**, **explain** them fully and give **examples**. Below is a list of points you may want to include in your answer:

◆ Petitions
◆ Using the media.

Remember: it is not enough to write a list, you must write **in detail**!

CREDIT

Describe, **in detail**, the **rights and responsibilities** of pressure groups.

(Knowledge and Understanding, 8 marks)

Questions and Answers continued ➢

Chapter 1

Questions and Answers continued

Point	One right that pressure groups have is to protest. However, clear responsibilities go with this right. Pressure groups have the democratic right to protest but they must not break the law while doing so.
Explanation	Pressure groups use this right in a number of different ways. They organise marches and demonstrations to show the strength of support for their cause. Their members also stage publicity stunts to put pressure on the government.
Example	For example, Fathers 4 Justice staged a number of high-profile demonstrations. However, they highlighted their lack of responsibility by breaking the law many times. This negatively affected their public image and, as a result, they had little chance of gaining the ear of the Government as an insider group.
Link	Therefore, Fathers 4 Justice did not act responsibly and as a result received a great deal of negative publicity.

The other points that could be used to answer this question are:
- The right to use the media – responsibility to be as accurate as possible
- The right to criticise the government – responsibility to be truthful.

Hints and Tips

You have come to the end of a section of work and it is time to organise your notes about Pressure Groups and add them to your information about Politics. Try to see how the two topics fit into Living in a Democracy and try to remember the concepts they illustrate.

Chapter 1

Trade Unions

Key Ideas

Workers have a **right** to join a trade union, elect their union **representatives** and **participate** in union activities. Trade unions, and their members, have a **responsibility** to behave reasonably and act within the law.

What You Should Know

You could be asked questions about the following information in the examination:

- rights and responsibilities of trade unions
- reasons for and against joining a trade union
- ways in which trade union members can participate in union activities
- ways in which trade unions represent their members
- role of a shop steward
- under-representation of women and ethnic minorities.

What is a trade union?

Trade unions are organisations that try to protect the rights of workers. They vary in size and membership although a common feature over the years has been the decline in trade union membership across the country. This used to be much higher. Trade unions are specialist pressure groups that focus on employers and employees.

Rights and responsibilities of trade unions

Rights	Responsibilities
Unions	
◆ To recruit members	◆ Not to put pressure on people to join
◆ To ask about changes in wages and conditions	◆ Not to make unreasonable demands or threaten
◆ To take industrial action to protect workers' rights, e.g. strike	◆ Hold a secret ballot to see if majority of members support the action; only take action that is peaceful and lawful
Members	
◆ To participate in electing shop stewards	◆ To vote in the election
◆ To have union representation in any dispute with management	◆ To report problems, e.g. health and safety issues, to the shop steward
◆ To take part in industrial action	◆ To act within the law, e.g. picketing (protesting outside the workplace) must be peaceful

Trade union membership

Reasons for joining a union	Reasons for not joining a union
Negotiate (discuss) better pay and conditions with employers.	Good pay and conditions so do not need unions to negotiate for them.
People are part of a group and, therefore, employers will find it difficult to 'pick on'/victimise their staff.	Wage rises are given to everyone; those who are not part of the union get the advantages without joining.
Legal backing and advice is available to employees.	Some people object to unions as they think they have too much power.

How trade union members can participate in union activity

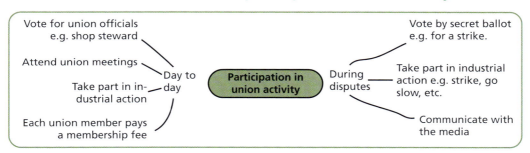

Figure 1.8 Memory map: participation in union activity

How trade unions represent their members

Methods	Description
Grievances	Take workers' complaints to management, and try to get the problem fixed. For example, if teachers were concerned about the temperature in their classroom, they could take their complaint to their EIS (Educational Institute for Scotland) union representative/shop steward.
Industrial action	If a settlement is not reached, a union may use industrial action **(striking)** to reach a **compromise agreement**. For example, the Fire Brigade Union went on strike to highlight their dissatisfaction with the pay deal they were offered by their employers. This action was relatively successful because they recieved a pay increase. However, it was not the amount they asked for and it was tied to changes to working practice. In other words, it was a compromise; both sides gave in a little to settle the dispute.
Services	Trade unions provide a range of services to their members, such as legal help on issues. For example, if a woman was unfairly dismissed **(sacked)** when she became pregnant, she could go to her union and ask for help in fighting the dismissal in an industrial tribunal.

Chapter 1

Shop stewards

Members of a trade union **elect** union representatives called shop stewards. Trade unions by law **must** be organised democratically. Elections are held for shop stewards and for trade union leaders. Almost all trade union decisions are made after a democratic vote. Shop stewards are **not paid** by their trade union, but they do receive an allowance for the work they do, e.g. travel expenses to a conference in London.

Description	Why is it important?
They **recruit** new members and collect subscriptions (this is the money people pay to be a member of a Trade Union).	They are the first point of contact a member has with their union. This ensures that the number of trade union members continues **to grow and feel supported.**
They **inform** workers of union decisions, e.g. a union may support a government policy like the National Minimum Wage (NMW).	This lets the union members know how the union is representing them. For example, the shop steward could hold a union meeting to inform members what action the union is taking to protect their rights under the NMW.
They take **grievances/complaints** to management on behalf of workers.	Management are more likely to treat grievances seriously because the shop steward represents all of the workforce who are union members.
They **negotiate** with management about wages and conditions, e.g. they make sure health and safety, and other employment legislation, is being adhered to (followed).	They give their members a more **powerful voice** when dealing with management because they potentially have the backing of the whole trade union movement. The relationship between employers and employees has a huge impact on working conditions. In the past, trade union pressure led to many improvements in wages and working conditions.

Questions and Answers

GENERAL

Describe **two** ways in which members can **take part** in trade union activities.

(Knowledge and Understanding, 4 marks)

Questions and Answers continued ➤

Questions and Answers continued

To answer this question fully you must make sure that you make **two points**, **explain** them fully and give **examples**. Below is a list of points you may want to include in your answer.

- Members can vote for the shop steward.
- Members can take industrial action.

Remember: it is not enough to write a list, you must write **in detail**!

CREDIT

Describe, **in detail,** the **rights and responsibilities** trade union members have during a dispute with their employers.

(Knowledge and Understanding, 6 marks)

In this example, you have to look very closely at the question. Don't just rush into it, and write everything you know about right and responsibilities of trade unions. You have to write about trade union **members** and about their rights and responsibilities **during a dispute**.

Think carefully about how you can use the information in your notes to answer this question. For example, a dispute does not just mean **industrial action**, although that is one right you can give; it also covers the right of union members to **raise grievances** with the management and to have **union representation** when they do so.

So you have three points that you can now **PEEL** – Point, Explanation, Example and Link!

 You might be given statistics about trends in trade union membership or how representative trade unions are. It is important that you know what these statistics show.

SYLLABUS AREA 1 – LIVING IN A DEMOCRACY

Chapter 1

Changes in trade union membership

Proportion of workers who are trade union members, UK 1995–2004			
	1995	2000	2004
All employment	35%	27%	28.5%
Gender			
Male	33%	30%	28.5%
Female	30%	29%	29.1%
Type of work			
Manual	33%	28%	30%
Non-manual	32%	30%	36%
Full-time/part-time			
Full-time	36%	33%	31.5%
Part-time	21%	23%	21%
Employment sector			
Manufacturing	34%	28%	28%
Services	33%	31%	33%

Hints and Tips

This is the kind of table where remembering **HINT – Heading, Information, Number and Trend** – is very useful. Looking at the **headings** tells you that you can get **information** not only about the proportion of all workers who are members of trade unions, but also about the proportion of men and women, manual and non-manual workers, full and part-time workers and manufacturing and service workers. The **number** is given as a percentage of the total of workers in the UK and because you are given information for more than one year, you can see the **trend** in trade union membership in the last ten years in the UK.

Use the table to make some notes about the changes in trade union membership in the UK between 1995 and 2004. This will give you examples that you can use in your KU answers.

How representative are trade unions?

Women

Percentage of trade union members and officials by gender, UK 2004	Male	Female
All trade union members	49.8%	50.2%
Shop stewards	52%	48%
Full-time regional officials	81%	19%
Full-time national officials	67%	33%
National executive committee members	68%	32%
General secretaries	83%	17%

The statistics show that women are under-represented in the full-time and elected positions in trade unions. Just over half (50.2%) of trade union members are women, but women account for less than half of the elected shop stewards and national executive members. Three-quarters of the full-time regional and national officials are men and only 17% of general secretaries are women.

The social and economic reasons for the under-representation of women in full-time and elected positions are given in the table below.

Social reasons	Economic reasons
◆ Some trade unions are dominated (controlled) by men. This makes it an intimidating (scary) place for women.	◆ Women are more likely to work part-time, so they are less likely to join a union, e.g. cleaners.
◆ Sexist men are unlikely to vote for a female shop steward.	◆ Women are more likely to be in low-paid work so might not be able to afford membership fees.
◆ Many women have family commitments so might not be able to give much time to union matters.	

Ethnic minorities

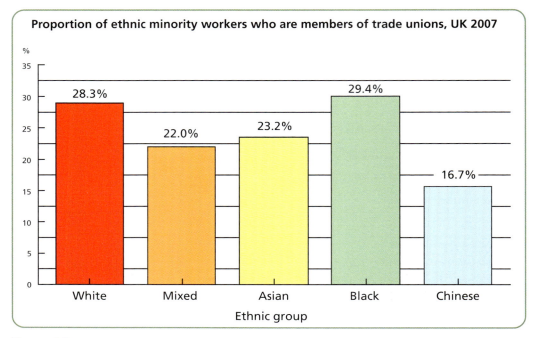

Figure 1.9

The chart shows that a higher proportion of black workers than white are members of trade unions. This is not surprising when you remember that the role of a trade union is to fight prejudice and discrimination in the workplace. Other ethnic groups have a lower proportion of trade union members, partly because a large number are self-employed or work in occupations and workplaces that traditionally have low union representation.

Percentage of trade union members by ethnic group, UK 2007	
White	93.4%
Mixed	0.5%
Asian or Asian British	3.0%
Black or Black British	2.1%
Chinese and other ethnic groups	1.0%
All	100%

Figure 1.10

When you look at the percentage of trade union members from each ethnic group, you see how under-represented ethnic minorities are. Only 6.6% of trade union members are from an ethnic minority.

Some of the social and economic reasons for the under-representation of ethnic minorities in trade unions are shown in the table below.

Social reasons	Economic reasons
◆ Racist members are unlikely to vote for an ethnic minority shop steward.	◆ Ethnic minorities are more likely to be self-employed or work for a family business, therefore there is no need for a union.
◆ Some ethnic minorities might feel intimidated going to union meetings because they are dominated by whites.	◆ They are more likely to be in low-paid work so might not be able to afford membership fees.

Hints and Tips

*Congratulations! You have completed a syllabus area and it is time to organise your notes about Trade Unions and add them to your information about Politics and Pressure Groups. Try to see how the whole syllabus area of Living in a Democracy fits together. Make sure you understand the concepts of **rights and responsibilities**, **representation** and **participation** and that you know where they apply in each topic.*

Chapter 2

SYLLABUS AREA 2 – CHANGING SOCIETY

This syllabus area focuses on the concepts of **need**, **equality** and **ideology**.

It can be divided into the topics of:

- The Elderly
- The Unemployed
- Families.

You can revise the topics separately but the question in the examination may cover more than one topic.

The Elderly

Key Ideas

The elderly have a set of physical, emotional and financial **needs** that increase with age. The growing numbers of elderly people in the UK make **equality** difficult because elderly people with a private income and family help can meet their needs more easily than those who rely on benefits. As a result of the difficulty in meeting the needs of the UK's ageing population there is a difference in **ideology** about whether the state or the individual should meet the needs of the elderly in the future.

What You Should Know

You could be asked questions about the following information in the examination:

- the elderly population
- how national and local government, private companies, voluntary groups and families can meet the needs of the elderly
- how the housing needs of the elderly are met
- care in the community
- how new technology can help meet the needs of the elderly
- difficulties meeting the needs of the elderly
- inequalities amongst the elderly.

Chapter 2

The **elderly** are those people who are entitled to claim **retirement pension**. At present, this is men of 65+ and women of 60+, but by 2010 the retirement age will be 65 for both men and women.

The elderly are an increasingly important sector in society in a number of ways.

Socially (relates to the community)	Economically (relates to money)	Politically (relates to the Government)
Many community facilities are now geared towards meeting the needs of the elderly.	Some elderly people have a lot of disposable income providing a large market for goods and services geared towards their needs. A greater population of elderly people places an extra burden on the state in terms of welfare provision.	The elderly make up a large proportion of the population who turn out to vote and this makes the 'grey vote' politically influential. For example, a representative of the Senior Citizens Unity Party won a seat in the Scottish Parliament.

Information about the size of the elderly population can be given as pie charts or bar charts in an Enquiry Skills question.

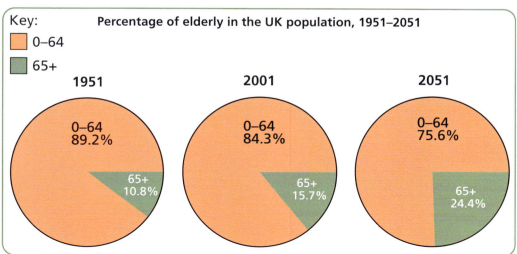

Figure 2.1

SYLLABUS AREA 2 – CHANGING SOCIETY

43

Chapter 2

> **Hints and Tips**
>
> When you are given statistics over a number of years, the **trend** is really important. Check if the numbers are rising or falling and make sure you comment on that in your answer.
>
> In this case the percentage of elderly in the population is rising. In 50 years' time, the elderly will be almost a quarter of the population.
>
> After you have noted the trend, try to think how it might affect our ability to meet the needs of a growing elderly population.

The elderly population is growing because people are living longer and this means there are more people in the 85+ age group. This is sometimes referred to as the **ageing population**.

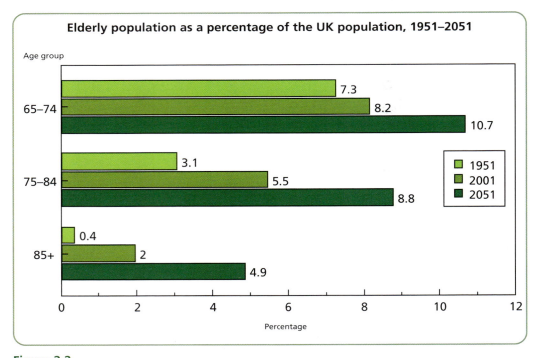

Figure 2.2

Hints and Tips

When you are given statistics over a number of years and divided into groups, look for the **trend** and **compare** the groups.

The **trend** shows the elderly increasing as a percentage of the UK population in all the age groups, but a **comparison** of the groups gives us more information.

The 85+ group is increasing much faster than the other groups – more than doubling in 50 years. Think about how this trend might change the needs of the elderly population.

Reasons for the growth in the elderly population

- Medical advances mean that formerly fatal diseases can now be treated.
- Better housing, living standards and diet mean that people are healthier.
- Working conditions and types of jobs have changed and fewer people do heavy manual work in poor conditions.

Effects of the growth in the elderly population

- Older people have more ill health; demand for health care will increase.
- The elderly are the most expensive group to treat; cost of NHS will increase.
- Retirement pension accounts for half the money spent on benefits; cost of social services will increase.
- The elderly (especially 85+ group) need home carers, sheltered housing, etc. – demand for these services will increase.

Problems created by the growth in the elderly population

The elderly are a **dependent** population; they rely on the working population to pay taxes to provide benefits and services. The birth rate is decreasing which means the working population is declining. In the future, the working population may not be large enough to provide money to meet the needs of the elderly.

Taxes might have to be raised to finance benefits and services for the elderly. Inequality will be created because some people will be able to afford private health care and housing while others will not.

Chapter 2

Meeting the needs of the elderly

Physical	Emotional	Financial
Needs that relate to a person's health and well-being	Needs that are fulfilled by having friends and loved ones around	Need for an income in retirement
National government provides:		
National Health Service – GPs, community nurses, free prescriptions, flu jabs, etc.	Help for people looking after an elderly person, e.g. an allowance for carers	State retirement pension – given to over 65s
Free personal and nursing care – provided by Scottish Government		Winter Fuel Payment – annual payment to help with heating bills
Local government provides:		
Community care – assistance to live in own homes	Home carers – housework, shopping and company	Reduced prices for council facilities
Adapting houses – mobility and security aids	Day care centres – low-cost meals and company	Council benefits, e.g. reduced Council Tax, Housing Benefit
	Sheltered housing – independence with security and company	
Private companies provide:		
Private health care like BUPA	Leisure facilities, holidays and other services, e.g. SAGA	Private pensions and investments
Mobility equipment and adaptations, e.g. stair lifts	Retirement flats and villages	Employment with companies like B&Q
Voluntary groups provide:		
Church organisations provide sheltered housing and homes	Meals on wheels staffed by volunteers from groups like WRVS	Groups like Age Concern provide grants for projects to help elderly and to campaign for better pensions and benefits
Family provides:		
Families offer their elderly relatives a home and help with mobility	Families provide care and attention	Families might offer financial assistance by helping out with bills

Meeting the housing needs of the elderly

Apart from the need for shelter, the elderly have additional needs in relation to housing. For example, some elderly people do not have enough retirement pension to meet the **cost** of rent or heating bills. Without heat, elderly people can develop **hypothermia** (dangerously low body temperature). As they get older, elderly people become more frail and can have **problems with mobility**. They may need the house adapted or help with household tasks.

- **Adapting existing housing**

    This may involve, for example, extending the house to provide a self-contained 'granny flat'; altering a two-floor house so that an elderly person need only use the ground floor for living; installing a stair lift, grab handles or a hoist in the bath to help with mobility; or building ramps, widening doors and lowering worktops if the elderly person is in a wheelchair.

    Elderly people who own their own home can sell that and buy purpose-built retirement housing. Facilities usually include a quiet location, people of a similar age living together, emergency alarms, repair services, lifts and wheelchair access and entry phones to control access to the building.

- **Sheltered housing**

    This meets the needs of many elderly people who are fit and independent enough to live on their own but who like the reassurance of having a 24-hour warden who checks on the safety of residents; social events such as coffee mornings; a communal lounge and organised outings; and design features like pull cords, two-way entry intercom, laundry facilities and personal alarms.

- **Residential homes**

    These provide care for elderly people who can no longer look after themselves. Needs are met with facilities like trained staff who are available 24 hours a day, handrails, lifting equipment in bathrooms, lounges for social activities and visits from hairdressers, library, etc.

- **Nursing homes**

    These provide additional support for those who are ill. Services include qualified nursing staff available 24 hours a day, call facilities in each bedroom for prompt attention, special diets, and visits from health professionals.

Care in the community

More elderly people are now encouraged to stay in their own homes as long as possible with the support of a number of services. Social workers assess their needs and draw up a **care plan** to meet these needs, using various services.

- **Day care centres and lunch clubs** – elderly people can attend, often with bus transport arranged. Meals are provided at a low cost. This helps by providing a balanced diet, reducing food costs and providing company.

- **Home carers and meals on wheels** – home carers (also known as 'home helps') clean, shop, wash and iron as well as providing company. Volunteers bring hot meals to elderly people's homes. Meals on wheels provide a balanced diet and cut food costs.
- **Community nurses and occupational therapists** – community nurses provide basic health care, and help with bathing, dressing wounds and giving injections, e.g. for diabetes. Occupational therapists supply equipment to make life easier, for example, grab rails, special baths and showers, lower work surfaces and cupboards, etc.

To help them feel more secure in their homes, many elderly people who live alone carry a remote control alarm system linked to the telephone which enables them to call for help at any time.

Care in the Community

Good points	Bad points
Independence is retained because the elderly can continue to live at home.	Some elderly people who remain in the community suffer injury and declining health because their needs have been inappropriately assessed or they have 'slipped through the net'.
Meets the needs of some elderly people because they have their own 'care plan' which identifies what they need and who will provide the care.	It is argued that some elderly people, who should be in residential care, are kept in the community because it is a 'cheaper option', i.e. it costs less than residential or hospital care.

How new technology can help meet the needs of the elderly

There are a number of new technologies currently available.

- New medical treatments and drugs.
- Medical technology like digital hearing aids, replacement hips and pacemakers.
- Mobility aids like stair lifts, electronic wheelchairs and bath lifts.
- Sensors and alarms to alert or call for help if an elderly person falls.
- Adaptations to make life easier in the home, e.g. remote controls, flashing lights for doorbells and telephones, sensors to switch on lights, etc. automatically.
- Many elderly use computers and email to keep in touch with family and friends. They also use the Internet for online information, entertainment and shopping.

New technology being developed includes:

- **Telemedicine**, where readings like blood pressure, glucose levels, etc. are taken at home and sent to the doctor's surgery by computer or mobile. Reminders to take medication and other instructions can also be relayed. This has also been called the 'hospital home' because it would cut down the number of visits needed to hospital or the GP.

◆ **Telecare**, where sensors and wireless communication throughout an elderly person's house can automatically switch on lights, heating and appliances, as well as giving reminders about medication and raising the alarm if no movement is detected. This would allow elderly people to remain independent in their own homes for longer.

Questions and Answers

GENERAL

> Some elderly people can have their **needs** met by their family.

Describe **two** ways in which the **needs** of some elderly people can be met by their family.

(Knowledge and Understanding, 4 marks)

To answer this question fully you must make sure that you make **two points**, **explain** them fully and give **examples**. Below is a list of points you may want to include in your answer:

◆ care and attention
◆ financial assistance.

CREDIT

> Elderly people have special housing needs.

Using examples, explain how the housing needs of the elderly are met by any **one** of the following:

◆ Local government   ◆ Voluntary organisations   ◆ Private companies.

(Knowledge and Understanding, 4 marks)

To answer the question, **PEEL** – give **two points**, **explain** them fully, give **examples** and **link** back to the question to show how your example meets a special housing need of the elderly. On the following page you will find some points you could include in your answer.

Questions and Answers continued ➢

Chapter 2

> **Questions and Answers** continued
>
> | Local government | Voluntary organisations | Private companies |
> |---|---|---|
> | ◆ Sheltered housing | ◆ Sheltered housing | ◆ Retirement flats/homes |
> | ◆ Adapting houses | ◆ Meals on wheels | ◆ Mobility aids |

Difficulties in meeting the needs of the elderly

Some elderly people have difficulty meeting their needs because:

- Retirement pensions are too low – prices keep rising (inflation) and when benefits are not increased in line with prices, the same amount of pension buys less.
- Some elderly people do not claim all benefits they are entitled to because:
  - they may view benefits as charity and have too much pride and independence to accept them
  - many elderly people are unaware of the benefits that are available
  - many pensioners refuse to give their private information on application forms
  - many benefits are means tested (e.g. Pension Credit) and the elderly are put off because they have to give details about the amount of money they have
  - application forms are confusing and can take a long time to complete.

The Government (state) is also finding it increasingly difficult to meet all the needs of the elderly because of the **ageing population**. At present the 'welfare state' (central and local government) provides for the elderly using the money the working population contributes by paying income tax, council tax and National Insurance. However, in the future the elderly population will grow while the birth rate will fall. This means that a smaller working population will have to look after a growing elderly population, and it may not be possible to meet all the needs of the elderly from taxation and National Insurance.

A decision will have to be made about who should look after the elderly and the country will have to decide whether to:

- increase taxation and National Insurance so that the welfare state can continue to provide for people in their old age

  or

- encourage people to take out private insurance and pensions during their working life which they will use to pay for their retirement.

Inequality amongst the elderly

Type of inequality	Examples
Physical	Some elderly people have greater health needs than others because:
	◆ health problems increase with age and elderly people over the age of 85 are more likely to suffer from age-related illnesses
	◆ some elderly people can afford to pay for private health care with quick access to treatment and are likely to have shorter spells of ill health.
	Some older people live in housing that does not meet their **needs** because the house is:
	◆ too big when children leave home or a partner dies
	◆ expensive to heat and repair on a limited income
	◆ unsuitable for those in ill health or with a disability
	◆ empty – lack of company and loneliness when an elderly person lives alone and has difficulty getting out and about.
Emotional	Some elderly people have greater emotional needs than others. For example, some elderly people:
	◆ feel worthless when they retire and do not try to change their lives; others see retirement as an opportunity to develop a new lifestyle
	◆ have the support of family and friends; others have little company or emotional support.
Financial	Some elderly people are less wealthy than others because they:
	◆ rely entirely on the state retirement pension which at its present level is too low to give a decent standard of living; others have a comfortable lifestyle because they have occupational pensions (paid by their former employers), private pensions (which they paid into when they were working), savings and investments or capital from the sale of a house as well as a state retirement pension
	◆ do not claim the benefits to which they are entitled; others have benefits like Pension Credit, reduced Council Tax and Housing Benefit to add to their basic state retirement pension.

Chapter 2

Questions and Answers

GENERAL

> *Some elderly people are better off than others.*

Give **two** reasons why some elderly people are better off than others.

(Knowledge and Understanding, 4 marks)

To answer this question fully you must make sure that you make **two points**, **explain** them fully and give **examples**. Below is a list of points you may want to include in your answer:

◆ private pensions, occupational pensions, savings, investments, capital from sale of house, benefits

◆ state pension, unclaimed benefits.

CREDIT

Explain, **in detail**, why some elderly people have greater health **needs** than others.

(Knowledge and Understanding, 6 marks)

Point	Some elderly people face greater health problems than others because of poverty.
Explanation	Those elderly people living on the poverty line are likely to suffer greater health problems like hypothermia because they might not have the money to pay for heating. Their diet is likely to be restricted to low quality foods that lack the nutritional value and vitamins that many elderly people need to combat health ailments like iron deficiency. In addition, their living conditions are likely to be worse, compounding their health needs because they might not be able to afford specially adapted equipment that could help with problems like mobility or arthritis.
Example	For example, many poorer pensioners in Clydebank live in tower blocks that exacerbate their health needs because problems with ventilation and insulation make heating expensive. Gang activity and related crimes in tower block flats can affect their mental health and lead to depression.

Questions and Answers continued ➢

Chapter 2

Questions and Answers continued

| Link | Therefore, low income and living standards can result in ill health. |

The other points that could be used to answer this question are:

- The older you are the more health problems you are likely to face.
- Elderly people who have a higher disposable income may be able to afford private health care.

Hints and Tips

You have come to the end of a topic and it is time to organise your notes about The Elderly. Make sure you understand the concepts of **need**, **equality** and **ideology**.

Chapter 2

The Unemployed

This topic focuses on the concepts of **need**, **equality** and **ideology**.

Key Ideas

The unemployed have financial, employment and training **needs** that increase with the length of unemployment, age, number of dependent children and speed of technological change. Central and local government, voluntary groups, private companies and individuals try to meet these needs but **equality** is difficult because employment opportunities vary around the country and groups like ethnic minorities, women, disabled people and older workers face barriers when trying to find employment. There are **ideological** differences about how much responsibility the state and the individual have for meeting the needs of the unemployed.

What You Should Know

You could be asked questions about the following information in the examination:

- regional unemployment and the North–South Divide
- causes of unemployment
- impact of new technology
- inequality amongst the unemployed
- effects of unemployment
- meeting the needs of the unemployed.

Regional unemployment – North–South divide?

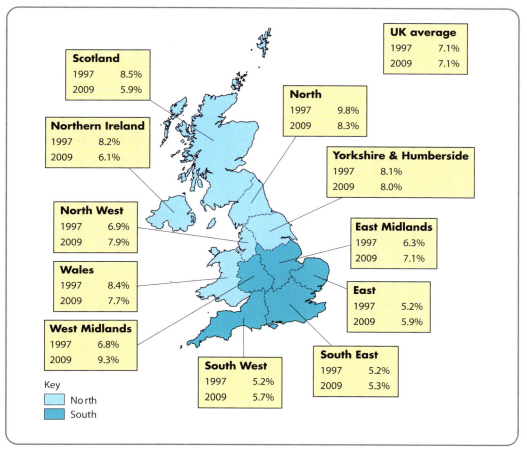

Figure 2.3 Regional unemployment in the UK, 1997 and 2009

Hints and Tips

You can use these statistics to assess if the UK still has a North–South Divide:

1. By comparing areas in the North and South with the UK average to show that unemployment is higher in the North, e.g. Yorkshire and Humberside is 0.9% above the UK average; South East is 1.8% below. This does not apply to all areas of the North, e.g. Northern Ireland and Scotland are below the UK average.

Hints and Tips continued ➤

Chapter 2

> **Hints and Tips** *continued*
>
> 2   By comparing North and South in 1997 to show that the North–South gap used to be bigger, e.g. 1997 unemployment in North of England is 2.7% above the UK average; South East 1.9% below.
>
> 3   By comparing percentage differences to show that the fall in unemployment has been greater in the North, e.g. unemployment in Scotland fell by 2.6% while it rose by 2.5% in the West Midlands.

Causes of unemployment

Structural – major changes in the types of jobs available due to competition from abroad, new technology or older industries closing down.

Cyclical – the economy goes into recession ('slump'). There is less money available, therefore less spending. Businesses cannot sell their goods, so workers are 'laid off' or made redundant.

The impact of new technology

Technology is the way people use discoveries and inventions to help meet their needs. New technology includes computers, robot machinery, fax machines, Internet, etc. It has changed the way people work and some aspects allow people to work from home:

- Broadband gives very quick and easy Internet access.
- Webcams provide face to face communication for people in different places.
- Fax machines allow documents to be sent all over the world.

People may wish to work from home for a variety of reasons.

- New technology allows more flexible working. This may suit people with young children as they can combine working with childcare.
- Self employed people can cut down the cost of commuting and the expense of premises by using their home as their base.
- Some jobs mean that you can stay in touch with colleagues through email without physically being in an office building. This can help those with disabilities or those who live in remote areas where travel is difficult.

Job Creation	Unemployment
New technology offers some groups of workers wider job opportunities, e.g. variety of home-based jobs such as freelance journalism.	New technology also destroys jobs, for example, in the manufacturing sector.
Large number of jobs created by 'hi-tech' industries in certain parts of Scotland, e.g. manufacture and assembly of components.	It puts off older workers who lack experience with technology.
New types of jobs created as a result of the 'footloose' nature of new technology, e.g. call centres.	'Footloose' industries can also leave a particular area and set up elsewhere, e.g. BT shut call centres and transferred the jobs to India.

Questions and Answers

CREDIT

> Some workers have more job opportunities from new technology than others.

For what reasons do some workers have more job opportunities than others?

(Knowledge and Understanding, 6 marks)

To answer this question fully you must make sure that you **PEEL** the question. Below is a list of points you may want to include in your answer:

- variety of home-based jobs
- hi-tech industries
- 'footloose' nature of some industries.

Inequality amongst the unemployed

Group	High unemployment because:	Difficult to get a job because:
Ethnic minorities	Prejudice and discrimination – not given a job because of their ethnic background (against Race Relations Act but still happens)	◆ Application form gives background and often not given an interview because of prejudice. ◆ May live in a poor area, have poor education and few qualifications. ◆ Society still does not accept ethnic minorities in positions of power; they may find it difficult to get managerial and other supervisory jobs.
Women	Family commitments and children mean they cannot work. Prejudice and discrimination means that women are not given certain types of jobs (against Sex Discrimination Act but still happens)	◆ Lack, or cost, of childcare means can only work part-time to fit in with looking after children. ◆ Society still does not accept women in positions of power; they may find it difficult to get managerial and other types of jobs. ◆ Many women, particularly lone parents, may not have completed their education and therefore have fewer qualifications.
Disabled workers	Prejudice and discrimination – employers think their disability will stop them from doing the job properly	◆ Employers may not have the facilities to employ a disabled worker. ◆ Employers may think that disabled people are not capable of doing a full day's work.
Older workers	Skills no longer in demand – considered too old by employers	◆ May need retraining – cheaper for employer to take on workers who already have the skills. ◆ Employers may think not worth retraining because will not get many more years of work.

SYLLABUS AREA 2 – CHANGING SOCIETY

Chapter 2

Group	High unemployment because:	Difficult to get a job because:
Younger workers	Lack work experience and qualifications	◆ Will need to be trained to do the job – employers would find it cheaper to employ someone who already has the skills. ◆ Lack experience and qualifications – if left school early may not have good qualifications; if older may have qualifications but no experience of the workplace.
Unskilled workers	Many former unskilled jobs now done by machines (many younger workers may also be unskilled)	◆ Do not have the necessary qualifications. ◆ Need training which is expensive and time-consuming so employers may prefer to take on a skilled worker.

You should make yourself familiar with the type of statistics that might be used in the examination to show inequalities amongst the unemployed.

The examples below will help you.

Gender

Total = number of men and women of working age signed on as unemployed. This shows that more males are unemployed than females. It gives numbers but does not show what proportion of the male and female working age population are unemployed.

Unemployment in the UK (October 2008)

	Total	Rate
Male	980,000	5.8%
Female	692,000	4.8%

Rate = percentage of males and females of working age who are unemployed. This shows that a higher percentage of males are unemployed than females. It also shows what proportion of the male and female working age population is unemployed.

Figure 2.4 Unemployment by gender in the UK

Age and gender

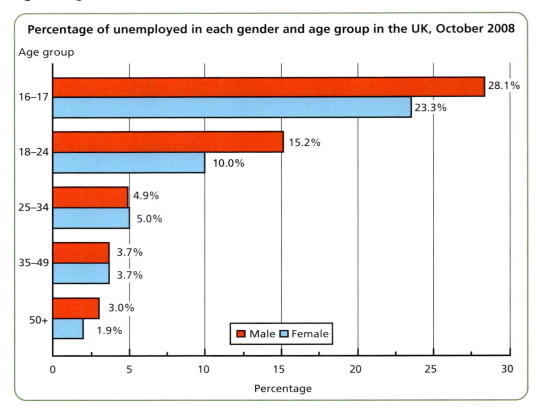

Figure 2.5 Percentage of unemployed in each gender and age group in the UK, October 2008

In almost all the age groups in the bar chart, the percentage of men out of work is higher than the percentage of women, although the gap between men and women becomes lower with age. Over a quarter of boys between 16 and 17 are unemployed – 4.8% more than girls of the same age. Between the ages of 18 and 24, 5.2% more males are unemployed and this reduces to 0% in the 35–49 year age group.

Ethnic minorities

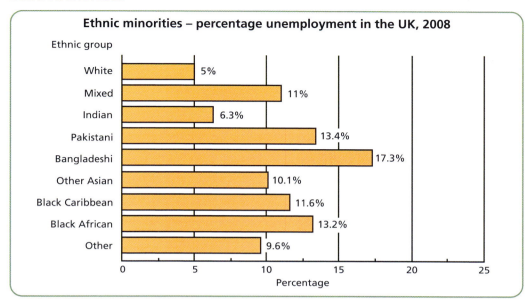

Figure 2.6 Ethnic minorities – percentage unemployment in the UK, 2008

The unemployment rate for all ethnic minority groups is higher than that of whites. For example, the Bangladeshi unemployment rate of 17.3% is nearly four times higher than that of whites.

Disabled

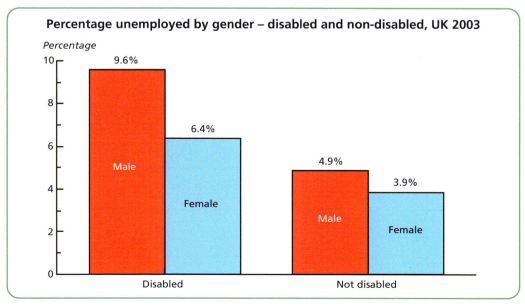

Figure 2.7 Percentage unemployed by gender – disabled and non-disabled, UK 2003

Chapter 2

More disabled men are unemployed than females – the unemployment rate for both disabled males and females is almost double that of people who are not disabled.

Questions and Answers

GENERAL

Give **two** reasons why **one** of the following groups might have difficulties finding a job:

- disabled
- ethnic minorities
- older workers

(Knowledge and Understanding, 4 marks)

To answer this question fully you must make sure that you PEE the question.

Effects of unemployment

National wealth	Lower because the government collects less money in taxes but has to spend more on unemployment benefits.
Income	Living standards fall because people rely on state benefits that are not enough to live on.
Health	People become anxious and stress can lead to illness. Lack of money means houses are not heated properly in winter and diet is poor. A culture of addiction can also develop as a way of trying to cope with the circumstances surrounding unemployment.
Social problems	Increased crime rate, family break-ups and financial problems as people borrow money and fall into debt when they cannot repay loans. Long-term unemployment can lead to social alienation which can lead to drug and alcohol problems.

When a large number of people are made unemployed it has a negative impact on an area. Think about the impact of a closure in your town, city or village. Think about some of the following:

- Skilled people may move away to find a new job.
- Shops will close.
- Amenities decline, e.g. bus services.
- Housing areas deteriorate.
- Vandalism, drug abuse and crime may increase.
- Employers are reluctant to set up business in degenerated (run-down) areas.

The closure of one large business or factory in an area can lead to **a domino effect** – that is, other businesses may suffer as a direct result.

Effects of unemployment on a local community

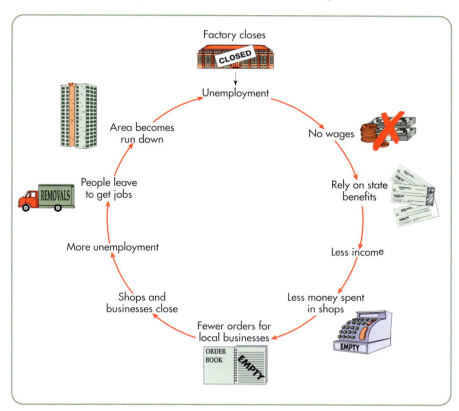

Figure 2.8 Cycle of deprivation

Meeting the needs of the unemployed

Financial (Money to support themselves and their families)	Employment (Help finding a job or other source of paid work)	Training (Develop skills to make it easier to find a job)
National government provides:		
Job Seekers Allowance (JSA) Benefit paid to the unemployed who are actively seeking work. Amount will vary according to circumstances of the person, e.g. single, married with kids.	**New Deal Phase 1** All New Deal clients (unemployed people) start with an interview at the local Job Centre Plus. A personal adviser will help them throughout their time on the New Deal. During the first four months the personal adviser will try to get the client into permanent work. The personal adviser will do this by arranging help with: ◆ applying for jobs ◆ attending interviews ◆ drawing up a CV.	**Skill-seekers** People aged 16–18 are placed on a scheme which provides a mixture of skills and on-the-job experience. They have to join to qualify for benefits. Some skill-seekers may be kept on by a company after the training period has ended.
	New Deal Phase 2 If the person is still unemployed after four months the adviser will discuss other options with them: ◆ self-employment ◆ voluntary work ◆ environment task force ◆ full-time education. There are different types of New Deal for various groups, e.g. New Deal 50+ catering for older unemployed people.	**Modern apprenticeships** These are aimed at school and college leavers. They are taken on by an employer and are paid either a wage or an allowance. The aim is to give the apprentice qualifications.
Local government provides:		
Council Tax Benefit – reduction in council tax. **Housing Benefit** – rent reduction.	**Get Ready for Work** – completing application forms; preparing for interviews. **Libraries** provide newspapers and Internet access free to find and apply for job vacancies.	**Adult education and literacy** – providing access to unemployed to improve literacy and qualifications. **Learning Centres** – training in word processing etc. to compile CVs and letters of application.
Other help:		
Voluntary groups like Citizens Advice provide information about applying for benefits. Unemployed people also work for voluntary groups to gain some job experience, work skills and references.		

Chapter 2

Questions and Answers

GENERAL

Describe two ways in which the Government helps to meet the **needs** of the unemployed.

(Knowledge and Understanding, 4 marks)

To answer this question fully you must make sure that you make **two points**, **explain** them fully and give **examples**. Below is a list of points you may want to include in your answer:

- financial benefits that help the unemployed person buy essentials
- training schemes that help provide unemployed people with the skills necessary to find a job.

CREDIT

Describe the ways in which **either** central government **or** local councils **or** voluntary groups help young people to find a job.

(Knowledge and Understanding, 6 marks)

To answer this question fully you must make sure that you **PEEL** the question. Below is a list of points you may want to include in your answer:

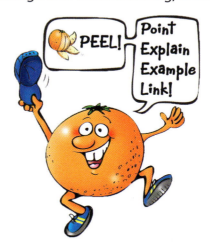

Central government
- Job Centre Plus
- New Deal 18+

Local councils
- 'Get Ready For Work'
- Free Internet access

Voluntary groups
- Prince's Trust
- Voluntary work

SYLLABUS AREA 2 – CHANGING SOCIETY

Chapter 2

Families

This topic focuses on the concepts of **need**, **equality** and **ideology**.

Key Ideas

Families have physical, emotional and financial **needs** that increase with the number of dependent children. **Equality** is difficult because some families have a level of income and family structure that helps them to meet their needs more easily. Central and local government, voluntary groups, private companies and individuals try to meet the needs of families but there is a difference in **ideology** about the extent to which the state should be involved.

What You Should Know

You could be asked questions about the following information in the examination:

- why some families have better living standards
- lone parents and employment
- meeting the needs of families
- national minimum wage
- working from home.

Types of families

Two main types of family group in the UK are:

- couple with dependent children
- lone parent with dependent children.

Dependent child – young person who relies on a parent or guardian for basic needs such as food, shelter, clothing, etc.

Married couple – man and woman, married and bringing up children. The most common family type in the UK; two-thirds of dependent children are brought up by married couples.

Dependent children: by family type, 2007, UK

Married couple	65%
Cohabiting couple	12%
Lone mother	22%
Lone father	2%

Cohabiting couple – man and woman living together and bringing up children but not married. This type of family is increasing in number.

Three-quarters of dependent children are brought up by couples.

Lone-parent – a woman, or a man, bringing up children on their own. A lone mother is the most common type of lone-parent family. Lone-parent families often start off as conventional couple families, but separation, divorce or death lead to the loss of one parent. Almost one-quarter of dependent children are brought up in lone-parent families.

Figure 2.9 Types of family

Why do some families have better living standards/lifestyles?

As with the elderly, there are many differences in the lifestyle of families, and it is wrong to stereotype them. For example, **not every** lone parent is poor. The lifestyles of families differ according to:

- **Income** – some families have several wage earners or wage earners in very well-paid jobs, while others rely on state benefits, or have no job. Lone parents may be in part-time employment with little prospect of promotion.
- **Health** – poorer families might have to live on a limited income. They may not be able to buy good-quality foods and their circumstances may also create the situation in which a culture of addiction develops.
- **Housing** – some families live in 'nice' areas with plenty of space, facilities, etc. while others live in run-down estates with poor-quality housing.
- **Family type** – families with two or more adults in the house are likely to find things easier than lone-parent households. In homes with more adults there is likely to be more money because more people will be working.

You should make yourself familiar with the type of statistics that might be used in the examination to show the living standards of families. The examples below will help you.

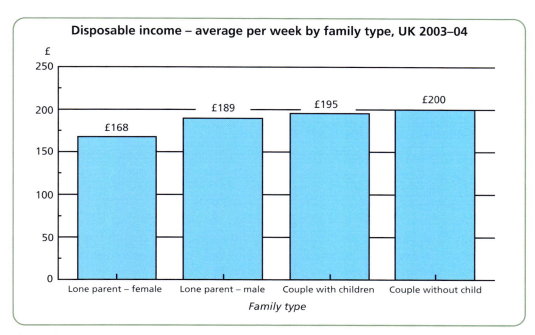

Figure 2.10

Lone parents have lower average disposable income than couples. Lone-parent families with a mother as head of the family have the lowest disposable income.

Earned income = money from wages, salaries and self-employment. Couples with children earn four-fifths of their income but only just over one-third of the income of lone parents is earned.

Social security benefits like Income Support and Child Benefit provide 41% of the income of lone parents. This is three times more than the percentage for couples with children.

Weekly income in the UK, 2003

	Earned income	Tax credits	Social security benefits	Pensions	Other
All households	63%	5%	19%	7%	6%
Households without children	69%	0%	7%	19%	5%
Couples with children	82%	3%	10%	2%	3%
Lone parents	37%	11%	41%	1%	10%

Tax credits = Child Tax Credit paid to all families with children and Working Tax Credit paid to parents in work; also includes help with childcare costs. Lone parents get just over one-tenth of their income from tax credits.

Over a half of the income of lone parents comes from state benefits, i.e. social security and tax credits.

Figure 2.11

Lone parents and employment

Lone parents usually have a low income because they find it more difficult than others to get a well-paid full-time job due to:

Working hours – lone parents with school age children may have to take a job that fits in with the school day and school holidays. This can be difficult because the working day is between 9 am and 5 pm and the school day is from 9 am to 3.30 pm. As a result, many lone parents are forced into low-paid, part-time employment with little prospect of promotion.

Childcare – it can be very expensive, or may not be available locally (or in the workplace). Pre-school children are given free nursery places but parents have to pay for childcare for school age children if they cannot find it within the circle of their family or friends.

Prejudice – some employers discriminate against lone parents because they fear that they may need to take time off to look after their children.

Chapter 2

Meeting the needs of families

Educational Maintenance Allowance

A weekly payment of up to £30 paid directly to young people from low income families who continue to attend full time education in school or college. EMA provides financial support by helping to pay for the cost of learning. This may improve their qualifications and therefore job prospects when they eventually leave.

Sure Start

A government initiative to provide the best start in life for every child, especially in the early years (0–3). It encourages close co-operation between education, childcare, health and family support to meet the needs of families with young children. Support is targeted at the poorest and most deprived areas of the country.

Child Benefit

Universal benefit paid to all families with children under the age of 16, or up to 19 if they are in full time education or training. It is not affected by savings or income (i.e. not means tested). It helps to pay the cost of raising children.

Tax Credits

Child Tax Credit and Working Tax Credit – these are means tested payments to ensure families are better off in work than on benefits. They help with the everyday cost of caring for children. They are paid directly to the main carer to make sure the money is more likely to benefit the children.

Child Trust Fund

A tax free savings and investment account set up by the government for each child born on or after 1 September 2002. The government puts £250 into the account to start it off, with a further £250 on the child's seventh birthday. Children in families with lower incomes will automatically get an additional government payment of £250. The account belongs to the child and cannot be touched until they turn 18, so that children have some money behind them to start their adult life.

National Minimum Wage (NMW)

The New Labour Government introduced the NMW which sets a minimum hourly wage rate. From October 2008 this was £5.73 per hour for workers over 22 years of age. The NMW improves and protects the earnings of low paid workers. It helps disadvantaged groups such as lone parents and ethnic minorities who tend to be in low paid employment.

SYLLABUS AREA 2 – CHANGING SOCIETY

Chapter 2

Questions and Answers

GENERAL

Give **two** reasons why some families with young children are better off than others.

(Knowledge and Understanding, 4 marks)

To answer this question fully you must make sure that you make **two points**, **explain** them fully and give **examples**. Below is a list of points you may want to include in your answer:

- Some families are headed by lone parents. This may mean that the family has a lower income.
- Some families have more children than others. It will be more expensive to look after four children than one.

CREDIT

Explain, **in detail**, why those with young children may find it difficult to find a job.

(Knowledge and Understanding, 4 marks)

Below is a list of points you may want to include in your answer:

- cost of childcare – low income
- problem in doing shift work or overtime.

Sometimes the questions in the examination do not specifically mention the elderly, the unemployed or families. This means you have to include information from more than one group to answer the question.

Hints and Tips

Congratulations! You have completed a syllabus area and it is time to organise your notes about The Family and add them to your information about The Elderly and The Unemployed. Try to see where information about the three groups connects. Make sure you understand the concepts of **need**, **equality** and **ideology** and how they apply to each group.

Chapter 3

SYLLABUS AREA 3 – IDEOLOGIES

This syllabus area focuses on the concepts **ideology**, **rights and responsibilities**, **participation** and **equality**.

There are two sections of examination questions for Ideologies:

- Section (A) – The USA
- Section (B) – China.

You must answer one section only – the section you studied! For most of you this will be Section (A) – The USA. However, if you have studied China, try following the headings we have used here to build your own notes.

The USA

Key Ideas

The USA has a democratic and capitalist **ideology**. People have the **right** to own businesses and **participate** at all levels of society but although America believes in **equality**, not all Americans have the same standard of living.

What You Should Know

You could be asked questions about the following information in the examination:

- rights and responsibilities in the USA
- protecting the rights of the American people
- reasons why Americans should participate in their political system
- ways, and the extent to which, Americans participate in their political system
- capitalism and the American economy

What you should know continued ➤

Chapter 3

> **What You Should Know** continued
> - population groups and immigration in the USA
> - types and extent of inequalities in the USA
> - tackling inequalities in the USA.

Rights and responsibilities in the USA

A **constitution** is a set of rules by which a country is governed. Part of the **American Constitution** is called the **Bill of Rights**; it lays out some of the rights and responsibilities US citizens have.

Freedom of Speech
Americans have the right to criticise their government if they disagree with its actions but they also have a resonsibility not to slander (lie) or make sexist or racist remarks.

Freedom of the Media
American TV, Radio and newspapers have the right to criticise the government but they also have a responsibility to respect the privacy of individuals and not libel (lie).

Right of Assembly
Americans can hold meetings, protest marches and demonstrations but they also have a responsibility to protest peacefully without violence or intimidation.

Right to Vote
US citizens over the age of 18 can vote in elections but they also have a responsibility to use their vote and accept their elected representative.

Right to Hold Public Office
US citizens can stand as candidates at local, state and national levels but they also have a responsibility to campaign legally and act honestly in office.

Right to Bear Arms
Americans have the right to own and, in some states, carry a gun but they also have a responsibility to keep the gun safely and only use it in self-defence.

Right to a Fair Trial
With a jury, defence lawyer and by not having to testify against yourself (sometimes called 'taking the Fifth'), Americans are guaranteed the right to a fair trial. Their responsibility is to obey the law and serve on a jury if called upon.

Figure 3.1 Rights and responsibilities in the USA

Protecting the rights of the American people

The American Constitution tries to make sure that no part of the government becomes too powerful. It does this by the **Separation of Powers** and by a system of **checks and balances**.

The job of government is split between **national** and **state** governments; this is called a **federal system of government**. Federal laws made by the national government in Washington DC are the same for the whole country, but state laws can differ, as the map below shows.

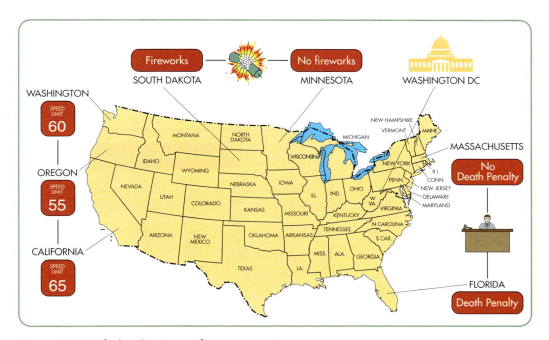

Figure 3.2 US federal system of government

There are **three** branches of national government:
1. The American parliament is called **Congress**. It is made up of two houses: the **Senate** which comprises (is made up of) 100 Senators, and the **House of Representatives** which comprises 435 Representatives. They make laws. This is called the **legislative branch**.
2. The **President** is elected separately; he/she is not a member of Congress. He/she chooses their Cabinet and administers (carries out) laws. The President serves a **maximum of 2 terms** (total 8 years). This is called the **executive branch**.
3. The **Supreme Court** upholds the **Constitution** and makes sure the President and Congress are acting within the Constitution. In other words, the Supreme Court ensures that laws are not broken by the Government. This is called the **judicial branch**.

Chapter 3

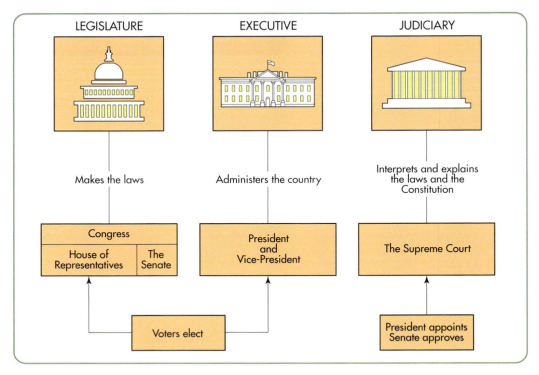

Figure 3.3 Separation of powers in the US Government

The **Supreme Court** protects the rights of the American people by making sure that all laws (state and federal) are constitutional. Americans who think a law takes away, or denies, their rights can challenge that law in the Supreme Court. For example, Supreme Court cases have protected the right to a lawyer (known as the 'Miranda Decision'), to 'one man, one vote', and the right of the media to publish government information that is in the national interest.

Questions and Answers

GENERAL

Describe **one** political **right** and **one** political **responsibility** that Americans have.

Remember: your right and responsibility must be linked.

In your answer you must use **American examples**.

(Knowledge and Understanding, 4 marks)

Questions and Answers continued ➢

Chapter 3

Questions and Answers continued

To answer this question fully you must make sure that you make **two points**, **explain** them fully and give **American examples**. Below is a list of points you may want to include in your answer. You must link these to the **Constitution of the USA**.

Rights

- To vote in elections.
- To have free speech.

Responsibilities

- To turn out and vote, accepting whoever the majority have chosen.
- To tell the truth, ensuring that you are not racist or prejudiced.

CREDIT

Describe, **in detail**, the ways in which the American Constitution protects the rights of the American people.

(Knowledge and Understanding, 4 marks)

This is an example of a question that is slightly different from what is usually asked. Being asked about how rights are protected by the Constitution might throw you a bit in the examination. If this happens to you – don't panic! Start with what you do know. You are likely to be prepared to answer a question about describing rights, so you should at least know what the Constitution is!

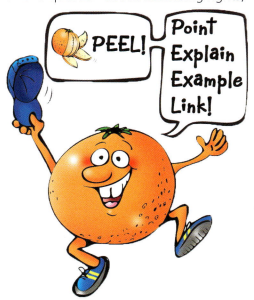

You can use **PEEL** (Point, Explain, Example, Link) to write your answer. Choose a right, for example the right to vote, give details, and an example, and link it back to the question by explaining how the Constitution guarantees the rights of Americans.

Of course, if you remember that the Constitution allows Americans to use the Supreme Court to protect their rights, you can use examples of rights that the Supreme Court has upheld.

Participation in the USA

Reasons why Americans should participate in their political system

- Americans can choose elected representatives who might solve their problems. They can choose the President they want to run the USA. For example, some Americans voted for George W. Bush as their President because they felt he would be harder on international terrorism.
- Americans can help an interest (pressure) group that is campaigning for something they are interested in. For example, pro gun supporters join groups like the NRA (National Rifle Association).
- If Blacks and Hispanics want more ethnic minorities in Congress they need to go out and vote for them, e.g. ethnic minority voting helped elect Barack Obama to President in 2008.
- Apathy ('why bother participating?') is a threat to democracy. Representatives are elected by only a few people, and special interest groups who can organise a lot of support become very influential. For example, the Christian Coalition mobilises support and raises funds for candidates.

Types of participation in the USA

Voting

America has more elections than any other country; over 1 million officials, from President to local mayor, are elected.

Opportunities to participate in elections in USA include:

federal elections for President every 4 years and Congress every 2 years (whole of the House of Representatives and one-third of the Senate)

state elections for Governor and State Legislature every 2 or 4 years

local elections for Mayor, City or Town Council and many other local posts like Sheriff, Police Chief, Fire Chief, School Boards, etc.

Standing as a candidate

People can stand as candidates for many of these elected posts. The large number of elected positions means that people from outside politics, who think they can make a difference, often participate. For example, Arnold Schwarzenegger was elected Governor of California.

Joining a political party

The main American parties are the Republican Party and the Democratic Party. Unlike British political parties, they are mostly local organisations, and only come together nationally every 4 years to choose and campaign for their candidate for President. They both want to appeal to a wide range of voters, so there is very little difference between them. However, the Democrats have more support from the poor, unemployed and ethnic minorities, while the Republicans are more closely linked to the rich, big business and the middle class.

By registering as a Democrat or a Republican, voters can participate in the **primary elections** which are part of the process of choosing the party's candidate for President.

Campaigning for a political party
The frequent elections in America, and the fact that a presidential election campaign lasts for a year, means that campaigning is very important to the political process. A US citizen/organisation may choose to support a political party financially. For example, the National Rifle Association (NRA) continues to spend millions of dollars to help the Republican Party win elections.

Joining and campaigning for an interest group
Americans can join interest groups (pressure groups) and participate in marches and demonstrations, and organise petitions, letter campaigns, media campaigns and other forms of lobbying in support of their cause.

Propositions
Some states allow people to put forward propositions on the ballot paper. Propositions are changes to state laws, which pass if a majority of the voters are in favour. For example, Proposition 227 in California ended bilingual education in state schools.

Hints and Tips

Although it looks familiar, rights and responsibilities and participation in the USA are different from those in the UK. Make sure you don't confuse the two. Use American terms like 'Congress'. To really impress the examiners, use examples like 'right to bear arms (guns)' and 'propositions', which only apply to the USA.

As you know, in all USA questions you are asked for specific American examples – but don't panic. Keep a few good examples in your toolbox and you should be able to apply these to a whole range of questions.

Chapter 3

Presidential election, 2008

A candidate needs 270 of the 538 Electoral College votes to win. Barack Obama got 365 Electoral College votes, so he was elected as President.

The winner of the popular vote in each state gets all the Electoral College votes for that state, so it is important for a candidate to win the big states, like California which has 55 Electoral College votes.

Barack Obama got just over half the popular votes.

Presidential election result, 2008

Candidate	Popular vote	% of popular vote	Electoral College votes
Barack Obama (Democrat)	67,066,915	52.7%	365
John McCain (Republican)	58,421,377	45.9%	173
Others (Independent)	1,653,986	1.2%	0
Turnout		62.8%	

The turnout in US elections is low; however, 2008 turnout was an improvement on other recent elections. For Congressional elections in non-Presidential Election years it is even smaller, as only about one-third of the electorate vote.

Presidential elections tend to be fought between the Republicans and Democrats. Third parties or independents do stand, but they find it difficult to compete.

Figure 3.4

Minority group participation

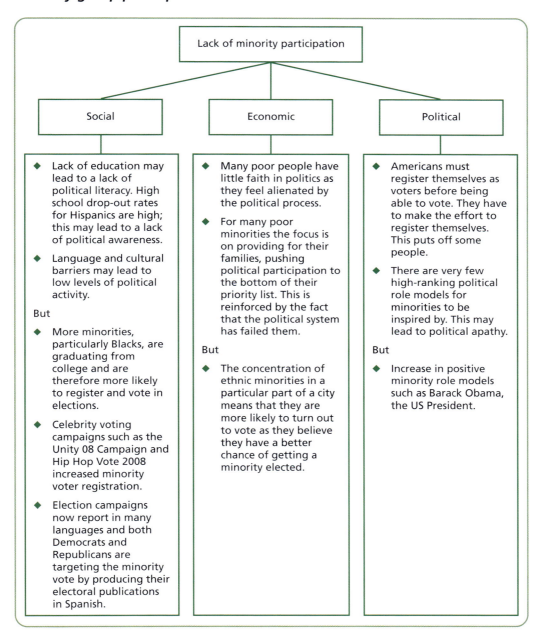

Figure 3.5 Minority participation

Chapter 3

Capitalism and the American economy

An ideology is a set of beliefs by which a country is run. America has a **capitalist ideology and economic system**. Many people believe that America's economic system works well because it has made the USA the richest country in the world and has allowed many Americans to have a very high standard of living. However, not everyone does well under capitalism. There is a great deal of **inequality**.

Capitalism means **free enterprise**. People can set up their own businesses, make a profit and use the money to expand their business or improve their living standard. Many Americans have achieved the **American Dream** by working hard. An example of someone who has achieved the American Dream is **Bill Gates**, who owns Microsoft; many other people have also achieved the American Dream.

Under capitalism, the Government encourages individuals to **look after their own affairs** and will only get involved when necessary; Americans do not have as wide-ranging free health care as we do in Britain. As a result many people choose to take out **private medical insurance**.

Questions and Answers

GENERAL

Describe **two** reasons why some Americans have started up their own business.

In your answer you must use **American examples**.

(Knowledge and Understanding, 4 marks)

To answer this question fully you must make sure that you make **two points**, **explain** them fully and give **American examples**. Below is a list of points you may want to include in your answer:

- To achieve the American Dream
- To make profits of their own so that they themselves benefit from their expertise or skill and so escape being paid low wages.

Remember: it is not enough to write a list, you must write **in detail**!

Population groups and immigration in the USA

There are just over **300 million** people in the United States of America. The population of a country changes over time, and so does its ethnic composition (make-up). The table below shows the **current** ethnic composition and the way it will have changed by **2050**. As you can see, African Americans, or Blacks, are no longer the second largest population group. There are approximately one million more Hispanics. We often refer to smaller sections of the population as **ethnic minority groups**.

Whites (66%)	Hispanics (15.1%)	African Americans (12.9%)	Asians and Pacific Islanders (APIs) (5.1%)	Native Americans (0.9%)
European immigrants	Spanish speakers from Cuba, Puerto Rica, Central and South America	Descendants of slaves and newer immigrants from the Caribbean	Japanese, Chinese, Koreans, Vietnamese and Pacific Islanders	Original population of America who are now a conquered minority

By the year **2050**, the **ethnic composition** (number of people from different groups) of America will change:

Whites (51%)	Hispanics (25%)	African Americans (15%)	APIs (8%)	Native Americans (1%)

This means that ethnic minorities will make up a bigger proportion of the US population.

Chapter 3

Types and extent of inequalities in the USA

You might be given statistics about inequalities in the USA. It is important that you know what these statistics show.

Selected social, economic and political indicators, USA 2005–09	White	Hispanic	Black	API
Housing				
Owner-occupiers	73%	46%	47%	54%
Education				
High school drop-out rate	7%	28%	13%	11%
High school graduates	85%	57%	78%	86%
College graduates	26%	11%	16%	44%
Health				
Life expectancy (years)	77	80	72	83
Health insurance	10%	32%	19%	17%
Money				
Unemployment	6%	9%	11%	5%
Average income	$54,920	$36,679	$33,916	$66,103
Poverty rate	8%	21%	24%	10%
Representation				
Senate	94	3	0	2
House of Representatives	365	28	41	4

Hints and Tips

This is the kind of table where remembering **HINT – Heading, Information, Number and Trend** is very useful. Use HINT to analyse this table and find information that you can use as strong examples in your answer to KU questions.

Chapter 3

Questions and Answers

CREDIT

Give **detailed** examples to illustrate that **social** inequality still exists in the USA.

In your answer you **must** use American examples.

(Knowledge and Understanding, 6 marks)

To answer this question fully you must make sure that you **PEEL** the question. We have provided part of the answer by focusing on housing as an example of social inequality. Below are further points you may want to include in your answer.

Health
- Blacks and Hispanics are less likely than Whites to have health insurance.
- Life expectancy is higher for Whites than for other ethnic groups.

Education
- African Americans and Hispanics are more likely to drop out of High School early.
- APIs are more educationally successful than any other ethnic group.

The Justice System
- Victims of crime are often from minorities.
- Many Blacks and Hispanics feel victimised by the American legal system.

It is not enough to write a list, you must write **in detail**!

Point	Social inequality can be shown by housing differences between Whites and ethnic minorities.
Explanation	Whites are more likely to own their own homes and live in better quality housing in more affluent suburbs on the outskirts of cities, while Blacks and Hispanics are more likely to rent housing in rundown inner city ghettos.

Questions and Answers continued ➤

SYLLABUS AREA 3 – IDEOLOGIES

Questions and Answers continued

Example	For example, less than half of Blacks and Hispanics own their own homes compared to three-quarters of Whites. The 'Vanilla' suburb of Brentwood in Los Angeles (California) is 80% White. This is in stark contrast to Watts in Los Angeles which has an 80% Black and Hispanic population. The majority of people in Watts live in public housing projects like Jordan Downs, which has the highest rate of violent crime in Los Angeles.
Link	These differences in housing show that social inequality between Whites and other ethnic groups still exists in the USA.

Tackling inequalities in the USA

The government of the USA has implemented many policies to tackle inequalities between different groups.

- **Affirmative Action** or positive discrimination measures in the 1970s and 1980s tried to reduce inequality by bringing in measures to help ethnic groups overcome discrimination.
- The **Opportunity Scholarship Program** and the **College Opportunity and Affordability Act** continue to support low income households, mainly minorities, with the cost of private schooling. They also provide greater funding for colleges serving low income and minority students.

The living standards of many ethnic minorities have improved as a result of these policies. They have made **social, economic and political progress**.

Social	Economic	Political
Less discrimination exists in education. **Better education,** especially for Asian and Pacific Islanders (APIs), has led to improved job prospects and greater earning potential. For example, in 2008 about one-third of APIs earned over $100,000 per year.	America is a **less racist** place than it was 50 years ago. Employers are now more likely to employ African Americans. Furthermore, **Affirmative Action** and other programmes have tried to tackle inequality.	There has been **increased representation** of ethnic minorities at all levels of Government. High-profile names include **Eric Holder**, Attorney General, and **Steven Chu**, Energy Secretary.

Reasons why inequality exists

Economic	Social	Political
The movement of whites from inner cities to suburbs is termed **'white flight'**. This means that whites pay taxes in different areas; as a direct result of this inner city areas suffer. This trend can also be seen amongst middle class African Americans, known as **'black flight'**. Recent governments have reduced **welfare (benefit) spending**. This has hit minorities harder as many rely on the benefit system due to the poverty cycle, or circle of poverty.	**Discrimination** still exists in jobs, housing and education. This has made it difficult to improve living standards. **Language problems** exist for many older members of the Hispanic community and many new **illegal** and **legal** immigrants. Many people from minority groups are stuck in the **'vicious circle of poverty'** from which they cannot break free. For young people there are very few positive role models, which can lead to a sense of disenchantment and disenfranchisement.	Most minorities feel that they have been failed socially and economically by the political system due to **low participation** and under-representation. Political parties cannot completely heal inequality because it will **cost too much**, and this would involve raising taxes which would be unpopular. Also, inequality relates to attitudes. Attitudes can only be changed through time and education.

Figure 3.6 The vicious circle of poverty

Chapter 3

Questions and Answers

CREDIT

Explain, **in detail**, why **social and economic inequality** exists in the USA.

In your answer you **must** use American examples.

(Knowledge and Understanding, 8 marks)

To answer this question fully you must make sure that you **PEEL** the question. Below is a list of points you may want to include in your answer:

- discrimination and racism
- language barriers
- white and black flight
- inequalities in education.

It is not enough to write a list, you must write **in detail**!

Hints and Tips

Congratulations! You have completed a syllabus area and it is time to organise your notes about the USA. Make sure you understand the concepts of **ideology**, **rights and responsibilities**, **participation** and **equality**. In particular, try to understand how ideology applies to the American system of government and economy. Make sure all the examples you plan to use in your answers are **American examples**!

Chapter 4

SYLLABUS AREA 4 – INTERNATIONAL RELATIONS

This syllabus area focuses on the concepts **need** and **power**.

It can be divided into the topics of:
- alliances
- politics of aid.

 You can revise the topics separately but the question in the examination may cover more than one topic.

 ## Alliances

Key Ideas

By joining alliances and co-operating with each other, countries can increase their **power** and meet their economic and military **needs** more easily.

What You Should Know

You could be asked questions about the following information in the examination:
- why countries join alliances
- why countries join the European Union (EU)
- how the EU can meet the needs of Scotland
- if more countries should be allowed to join the EU
- why countries join the North Atlantic Treaty Organisation (NATO)
- if we should keep NATO
- NATO's new role
- how the UN tries to resolve conflicts
- how international organisations can resolve conflicts
- example of an area of conflict in Europe and abroad.

Chapter 4

Why countries join alliances

An **alliance** is a group of countries that join together and co-operate with each other to become richer and safer. Countries join alliances to trade, sign treaties and pool their resources to help meet the economic and security needs of their country.

Economic needs	Security needs
Basic needs (food, clothing, shelter) Employment Improved living standards	Safety from attack Able to defend their own interests Able to protect their own people
By joining alliances countries can …	
… trade with other countries and ◆ get goods they do not produce themselves ◆ sell their goods to a bigger market. Living standards improve because businesses produce more and take on more workers.	… co-operate with other countries and ◆ have a stronger defence by joining with their armed forces ◆ have a safer world by resolving conflicts and keeping the peace. Security improves because if a member state is attacked all other members will come to its defence. This is called 'collective defence'.
Countries can meet more needs collectively in an alliance than they can do individually.	
European Union (EU) 27 members in a single market with no trade barriers. The UK can buy and sell to a market of about 500 million people.	**North Atlantic Treaty Organisation (NATO)** 29 members help keep the peace in Europe and will come to the defence of any member who is threatened. **United Nations (UN)** 192 countries who keep peace in the world and promote friendly relations between countries by solving problems.

The European Union (EU)

The EU is an organisation of democratic countries set up in 1957 to improve living standards and prevent conflict in Europe.

It now has 27 members, an elected Parliament, a Council and a Commission that make decisions about how to meet the economic, social and political needs of member countries.

Why countries want to join the EU

The information in the following table can be used to answer questions about the benefits of being a member of the EU and reasons why more countries want to join the EU.

Chapter 4

SYLLABUS AREA 4 – INTERNATIONAL RELATIONS

Social Reasons	Economic Reasons	Political Reasons
Help for poorer areas	**Trade and jobs**	**Security and defence**
◆ Deprived areas of member countries get help from the Regional Development Fund to regenerate the area. ◆ Money is available for improving infrastructure, investment and education and training.	◆ There are no barriers to trade so member countries can buy and sell to a single market of about 500 million customers. ◆ The Common Fisheries Policy supports jobs dependent on fishing.	◆ Rapid Reaction Force helps with humanitarian aid, rescue missions and peacekeeping in Europe. ◆ It helps prevent conflicts between countries that are members of the same alliance. Countries are less likely to fight each other if they are connected to each other.
Reducing inequality	**Agriculture and food**	**Human rights**
European Social Fund provides help to member countries to reduce the gap between rich and poor areas of the EU.	Common Agricultural Policy (CAP) gives farmers a decent standard of living in return for stable food supplies and prices.	EU promotes the four freedoms of movement – goods, services, people and capital – as well as equal rights and the rule of law.

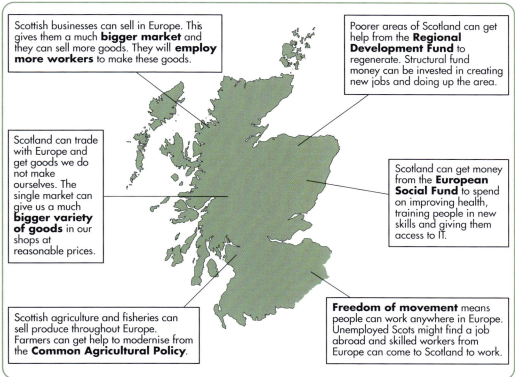

Figure 4.1 How the EU helps to meet the needs of Scotland

89

Chapter 4

Should more countries be allowed to join the EU?

In the years after the Second World War, six European countries got together because they wanted to prevent another major European war happening. They believed that if countries co-operated with each other it would make war less likely. They also wanted to improve the standard of living of their people after the suffering of the war.

In 1957 France, West Germany, Italy, Belgium, Netherlands and Luxembourg joined together to develop economic, social and political ties. Britain joined in 1973 and since then more and more countries have joined the EU. The biggest **enlargement** was in 2004 when ten new countries joined, taking the total to 25 and creating a market of about 450 million people. In the future it is likely that the number of countries in the EU will grow. In 2007 a further two countries joined – Bulgaria and Romania.

There are two ways the EU could expand: it could **widen** or **deepen** membership. So far it has opted to widen. This really means it includes more countries but does not take away the powers of member states. If the Union were to deepen that would take more power away from existing member states. This would give the EU greater control over member states. For example, at the moment the UK does not want to join the Euro currency system because it does not want to lose its economic identity.

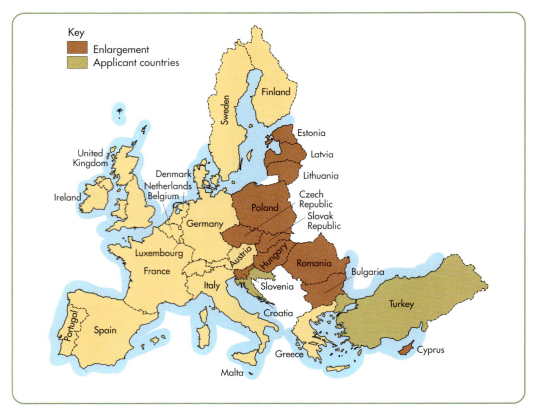

Figure 4.2 Enlargement of the EU

Chapter 4

SYLLABUS AREA 4 – INTERNATIONAL RELATIONS

Advantages	Disadvantages
For current members:	For current members:
◆ New markets to sell their products. ◆ Access to a cheaper workforce. ◆ Greater peace and security for Europe.	◆ Less chance of getting EU grants and subsidies because new members may be poorer. ◆ Possible influx of migrant workers, which may lead to racial tension.
For new members:	For new members:
◆ Access to EU funds and grants. ◆ Chance to improve their standard of living. ◆ Businesses may set up factories in new member states.	◆ The threat of inexpensive competition from another member state may cause the closure of businesses and higher unemployment.

Questions and Answers

GENERAL

Give **two** reasons to explain why some countries have recently joined the European Union.

(Knowledge and Understanding, 4 marks)

To answer this question fully you must make sure that you PEE the question. Below is a list of points you may want to include in your answer:

- ◆ free movement of people
- ◆ money available for poorest regions in the EU.

CREDIT

Explain, **in detail**, reasons both for and against European Union membership expanding.

(Knowledge and Understanding, 8 marks)

To answer this question fully you must make sure that you **PEEL** the question. On the following page there is a list of points you may want to include in your answer.

Questions and Answers continued ➢

91

Chapter 4

> **Questions** and **Answers** continued
>
> **For**
>
> - single market
> - more frequent communication between countries
> - freedom of movement for people
>
> **Against**
>
> - funds being diverted to 'new' poorer countries
> - cost of CAP
> - racial conflict

North Atlantic Treaty Organisation (NATO)

NATO was set up in 1949 to stop the spread of communism to Western Europe. It was based on **collective defence** and if one NATO member was attacked all other NATO members would come to its aid. This meant US forces would help Western Europe.

NATO was set up at the start of the **Cold War** when Europe divided into **communist** and **capitalist** countries. The former Soviet Union set up the **Warsaw Pact** with the communist countries of Eastern Europe.

Until the 1990s, the two military alliances faced each other and built up their weapons in a dangerous arms race. Since then communism has collapsed in Eastern Europe, the Warsaw Pact has disbanded and some of its former members have joined NATO.

Why countries want to join NATO

Collective defence – member states are protected by the other members. All will come to the aid of a member if they are attacked; the USA, Britain and France have nuclear weapons.

Shared defence – no single country needs all the military options. Countries can specialise and share the costs.

Security – NATO is the most powerful military group in the world, so members feel secure. Members also help each other in the fight against international terrorism. This has become particularly pronounced in the current international climate.

Co-operation – with most of the countries of Europe in the alliance, conflict between European countries is less likely. NATO Response Force (NRF) deals with conflicts quickly.

New members – new members, like Croatia and Georgia, see NATO as security against the re-emergence of communism and the threat of invasion. They also consider it confirmation of their transformation to democratic, capitalist countries.

Hints and Tips

This information can also be used to answer questions about benefits of being a member of NATO and reasons why more countries want to join NATO.

Should we keep NATO?

Yes	No
◆ NATO has kept the peace in Europe for over 50 years. ◆ Conflicts still happen in Europe and communism could re-emerge. ◆ NATO has a new role as a peacekeeping force in the fight against terrorism.	◆ The Cold War is over and communism is no longer a threat. ◆ Cost – unnecessary defence spending could be used on social services, health, etc. This is called the 'peace dividend'. ◆ EU and UN could do what NATO does.

NATO's new role

Defence – NATO now sees instability in any part of Europe as a threat to members and is prepared to take action 'out of area' to stop this. NATO, as part of the War on Terrorism, supports the government in Afghanistan in its fight against the Taliban.

Security – NATO sees expanding its membership to Eastern Europe as a way of increasing the security of Europe. It set up the Partnership for Peace to encourage links with former communist countries and ten years later several of them are members of NATO.

Counter-terrorism – NATO declared the 11 September attacks on the US an attack on all members and introduced measures to combat terrorism. NATO warships patrol the Mediterranean and a NATO Response Force is prepared to deploy quickly to any trouble-spot. NATO troops took part in their first 'out of Europe' action in Afghanistan in 2003. However, the invasion of Iraq caused a split, with some NATO countries, like the UK, taking part while France and Germany declined.

Chapter 4

Questions and Answers

GENERAL

Give **two** reasons why some people believe that European countries still need the NATO alliance.

(Knowledge and Understanding, 4 marks)

To answer this question fully you must make sure that you **PEE** the question. Below is a list of points you may want to include in your answer:

◆ benefits of collective and shared defence
◆ ability to meet new threats.

CREDIT

Explain, **in detail**, why some Eastern European countries feel that joining NATO could help meet their needs.

(Knowledge and Understanding, 4 marks)

To answer this question fully you must make sure that you **PEEL** the question. Below is a list of points you may want to include in your answer:

◆ collective and shared defence to meet security needs
◆ confirmation of move to democracy.

The United Nations

The UN has 192 members. It was set up in 1945. It is a world organisation which tries to promote world security, justice, welfare and human rights by providing aid to developing countries, through its **specialised agencies**, and by settling disputes **peacefully**.

Actions international organisations like the UN and NATO can take to resolve conflicts

Economic actions	Military actions
Sanctions – UN can ask members not to trade with groups involved in a conflict or to supply weapons to them. They hope that groups will respond to these sanctions by stopping the conflict. For example, trade sanctions are applied against Iran and North Korea for nuclear proliferation.	**Military action** such as the NATO bombing of Serbia, or sending in ground troops, or covert action when special forces carry out precision raids on predetermined targets. The UN does not have its own army; it relies on member countries.
Boycott of goods – member countries can be asked to deliberately avoid buying products that come from a particular country.	**Blockades** – to physically cut off access to a country by using troops and warships.
Cut-off aid projects, to halt the development of the country in question.	**No fly zones** – to prevent aircraft from getting in and out of the country.

The aim of these actions is to put pressure on the governments involved to change their policies and get involved in moves towards peace like:

Cease-fires – a cease-fire is an agreement to stop fighting so that negotiations can take place. The UN acts as a mediator by getting both sides to agree to try to end the conflict.

Peace talks – the UN tries to get all sides to talk on neutral territory and agree to resolve the conflict.

Peacekeeping troops – member countries send troops under the UN banner to make sure all sides carry out, and keep to, the peace plan.

Dealing with Security Threats and Terrorism

The attack on the Twin Towers in New York on 11 September 2001 and attacks in Madrid, London and Glasgow Airport by supporters of Islamic fundamentalist groups, like **Al-Qaeda** (the Base), and its organiser, **Osama bin Laden**, increased the need for countries to take measures to defend themselves from security threats and terrorist attacks.

Actions countries can take to deal with security threats and terrorism

- **Improve their internal security measures.**

  For example, the UK has:
  - Increased airport security with armed police, reduced hand luggage, Border Agency screening passengers with facial recognition technology, biometric passports, metal detectors, etc.
  - Various **Terrorism Acts** dealing with 'glorifying' and training for terrorism as well as committing terrorist acts. Suspects can be detained for 28 days before being charged and monitored after release.

- **Improve intelligence gathering and policing.**
  For example:
  - MI5 has doubled in size and actively recruits minorities.
  - Britain is a member of EUROPOL and INTERPOL.
- **Join international organisations like the EU, NATO and the UN.**

EU and UN Counter-Terrorism Measures
Member countries of the EU and UN increase their power by acting together to:

Prevent – stop spread of radical views, particularly via the Internet, and deny access to finance and weapons.

Protect – reduce target opportunities by improving border, transport and communications security and improving capability to deal with attacks.

Respond – investigate and bring terrorists to justice but also ensure respect for the rights of minorities.

NATO Counter-Terrorism Measures
Prevent – through **Terrorist Threat Intelligence Unit** at NATO headquarters in Brussels, member countries share information about suspected terrorists and potential plots.

Protect – ships of member countries carry out anti-terrorist patrols in the Mediterranean under **Operation Active Endeavour**. They escort non-military ships and also stop and board suspicious boats to search for drug dealing or human trafficking because these illegal activities often fund terrorism. NATO Airborne Early Warning and Control Aircraft (AWACS) patrol the skies during important international events like summits and sporting events like the 2004 Olympic Games in Athens.

Respond – member countries contribute land, sea, air and Special Forces to the **NATO Response Force**. Its 25,000 troops can be deployed within five days as an 'an initial entry force' giving time for larger forces to follow-on.

Afghanistan
After the 11 September terrorist attacks in 2001, the US **Operation Enduring Freedom** moved against **Al-Qaeda training camps** in Afghanistan and the **Taliban** government for refusing to hand over **Osama bin Laden**. In 2004, **Hamid Karzai** became the elected president of Afghanistan but the Taliban was not completely defeated and has been growing in strength, particularly in the south of the country in provinces like Helmand.

The EU, UN and NATO come together in Afghanistan to prevent, protect and respond to the threat of the Taliban and its support for terrorist groups.

Prevent – denying the Taliban finance from trade in narcotics, particularly opium. For example, the UK operates the **Helmand Food Programme** encouraging farmers to grow wheat instead of opium.

Protect – **European Union Police Mission** in Afghanistan (EUPOL) trains and monitors Afghan police to improve the security of border crossings. NATO helps the Afghan government in its policy of **Disarming Illegally Armed Groups** (DIAG) while the UN provides **support for democratic elections** in Afghanistan and promotes **human rights**, particularly for women.

Respond – NATO has a mandate from the UN to provide **International Security Assistance Force** (ISAF) in Afghanistan which conducts security and stability operations, supports the Afghan National Army and police with training and equipment, and provides humanitarian aid like food, shelter and medicines as well as the repair of buildings and infrastructure after military operations.

Questions and Answers

GENERAL

Describe **two** ways that European countries have been involved in recent international conflicts.

(Knowledge and Understanding, 4 marks)

To answer this question fully you must make sure that you **PEE** the question. Below is a list of points you may want to include in your answer:

- British troops in Afghanistan and Iraq
- trade sanctions.

CREDIT

Describe, **in detail**, some of the security measures which European countries have taken to protect themselves against international terrorism.

(Knowledge and Understanding, 6 marks)

To answer this question fully you must make sure that you **PEEL** the question. Below is a list of points you may want to include in your answer:

- new terrorism laws
- identification card schemes
- increased security at airports/rail stations.

SYLLABUS AREA 4 – INTERNATIONAL RELATIONS

Chapter 4

Hints and Tips

You have come to the end of a section of work and it is time to organise your notes about Alliances. Make sure you understand the concepts of **need** and **power**.

Politics of Aid

Key Ideas

Aid is given to help developing countries meet their **needs**. Giving aid can increase the **power** of developed countries.

What You Should Know

You could be asked questions about the following information in the examination:
- the differences between developed and developing countries
- the problems and needs of developing countries
- how needs of developing countries can be met through
  - international aid
  - UN specialised agencies
- why developed countries give aid
- how developed countries can increase their power through aid
- the factors developed countries take into account before they give aid and how they can benefit from giving aid
- the types of aid given and whether it really meets the needs of the people in developed countries.

All examination questions on the Politics of Aid require you to produce an example from the continent of Africa, not including South Africa.

The world can be divided into developed countries and developing countries.

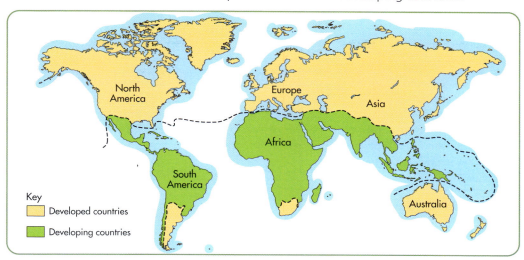

Figure 4.3 Developed and developing countries

	Developed countries	Developing countries
Terms:	Rich, North, First World, more economically developed countries (MEDCs)	Poor, South, Third World, less economically developed countries (LEDCs)
Countries (examples):	UK, USA, Japan, Australia, Spain	Sudan, Ethiopia, Chad, Zimbabwe, Uganda
Development indicators:	Low birth rate, low death rate and infant mortality, high life expectancy, high literacy rates, high GNI (wealth)	High birth rate, high death rate and infant mortality, low life expectancy, low literacy rates, low GNI (wealth)

The problems of developing countries

Social	Economic	Political
Population growth/ lack of food	**Debt/Trade**	**Civil war**
◆ High birth rate ◆ Fertile land used to grow cash crops for export ◆ Drought reducing the amount of land for growing food	◆ Large sums of money borrowed ◆ Has to be paid back with interest ◆ Poor terms of trade means many African countries cannot afford to do this	◆ Disputes over land, ethnic and religious differences ◆ Farmers forced off the land, crops destroyed, money spent on weapons
Poor health/education	**Poverty**	**Dictatorship**
◆ Not enough money spent on health and education ◆ Too few doctors, teachers, hospitals and schools	◆ A lack of economic development ◆ Corrupt governments misusing resources	◆ Little history of democracy ◆ Many were colonies of countries in Europe

All developing countries have some, or all, of these problems and as a result have the following needs.

The needs of developing countries

Social	Economic	Political
◆ Controlled population growth ◆ Improved agriculture and food production ◆ Better education and health care	◆ Debt cancellation ◆ Better terms of trade ◆ More economic development	◆ More stable democracies ◆ Ban on sale of weapons ◆ Effective peace keeping

Meeting the needs of developing countries

International aid

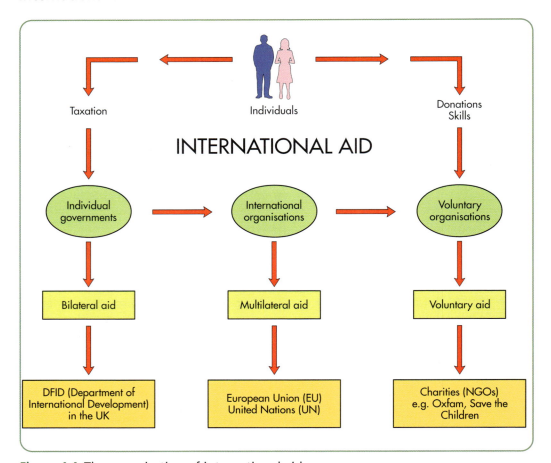

Figure 4.4 The organisation of international aid

Type of aid	Description/Example of aid project
Bilateral One government to another	The recipient usually develops a long-term relationship with the donor country. Britain's bilateral aid is organised by the Department for International Development (DFID).
	Meeting health needs in Tanzania **'Smitten not bitten'** The UK provides money to Tanzania through the DFID for Smartnets – mosquito nets treated with insecticide. This project has reduced the number of malaria cases in children under 5 by 10%. This is one of the eight Millennium Development Goals set by the UN.
Multilateral Aid given by international organisations	Multilateral aid is given by international organisations like the European Union (EU) and United Nations (UN) to the governments of poorer countries.
	Meeting employment needs in Ghana **GRATIS** The EU provides aid to GRATIS (Ghana Regional Appropriate Technology Industrial Service) which gives loans and trains people to start up small businesses making and selling local products. Gratis trains 8,000 people a year.
Voluntary Aid given by charities and NGOs	Projects are smaller scale, meeting local needs, but they often link into larger projects run by bilateral and multilateral agencies. Many charitable organisations such as Jubilee 2000 and Make Poverty History have highlighted the huge international support for debt cancellation in less economically developed countries.
	Meeting education needs in Sudan **Education on the go** Oxfam helps nomads, especially women, in Sudan learn on the move by providing 40 sheep as payment for a teacher. The community pays another 10 sheep a year and the teacher moves with the community and teaches in the open air.

UN specialised agencies

United Nations Children's Fund (UNICEF)

UNICEF helps to meet the education and health needs of people by providing:

- textbooks, blackboards, pencils, notebooks, and even tents for temporary classrooms
- safe water, immunisation and mosquito nets to protect children from malaria-carrying mosquitoes.

*Aid project: meeting education needs (**School in a Box**)*

These kits enable local people to educate children with basic materials. They have also been delivered to centres that provide care and support for orphaned and vulnerable children.

World Health Organisation (WHO)

WHO helps to meet the health needs of people by providing:

- information and training about health problems and how to deal with them
- immunisation campaigns to wipe out killer diseases like TB.

*Aid project: meeting the need for better health care (**Anaemia Programme**)*

Anaemia is an iron deficiency which can cause lethargy and in extreme cases can cause high infant mortality rates. WHO has provided iron supplements for pregnant women.

Food and Agricultural Organisation of the United Nations (FAO)

FAO is an agency which aims to meet the food needs of people throughout the developed and developing world.

- It aims to ensure that people have access to the quantity and quality of food required for them to live a healthy life.
- It works to improve nutrition and food production, and provides assistance to people in vulnerable rural areas.

Chapter 4

Aid project: meeting the needs of farmers in the war-torn Democratic Republic of the Congo

Local farmers and fishermen are helped to return to farm and fish in the areas from which they had fled during the war. The programme provides them with tools, seeds and livestock to allow them to re-start local food production and reduce dependency on food rations.

Questions and Answers

CREDIT

Describe, in detail, the ways in which UN aid helps to meet the needs of some African countries.

(Knowledge and Understanding, 6 marks)

To answer this question fully you must make sure that you **PEEL** the question. Below is a list of points you may want to include in your answer:

- UNICEF – meeting the education need through School in a Box
- FAO – meeting the needs of farmers in the Democratic Republic of the Congo.

Point	One way in which UN aid helps to meet the needs of some African countries is through the expertise of UNICEF, a key specialised agency.
Explanation	UNICEF specialises in delivering essential aid to benefit children. UNICEF aid meets social needs such as good-quality education and health care. It does this by providing numerous educational materials and resources like textbooks, blackboards and even tents for temporary classrooms.
Example	School in a Box has greatly benefited many Tanzanian children by providing them with the essential education needed to gain highly skilled employment with a good standard of living.
Link	Inevitably the country will benefit in the long term as people who have taken advantage of UNICEF's aid may help the country become more economically successful by providing skills and products that they can trade.

SYLLABUS AREA 4 – INTERNATIONAL RELATIONS

Chapter 4

Why developed countries give aid

Developing countries have difficulty in meeting their needs. As a result they require aid from developed countries.

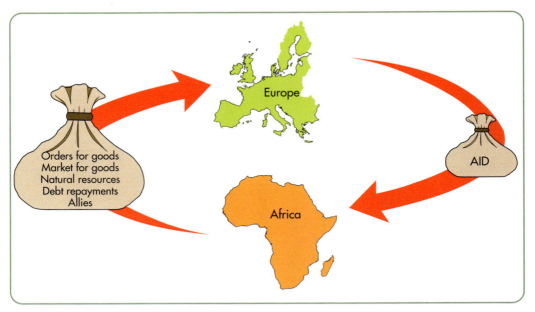

Figure 4.5 The flow of aid

Social reasons
- As a richer, developed country Britain feels it has a **responsibility** to help to improve the standard of life in poorer countries.
- British doctors, teachers, nurses, technicians, etc. who work in developing countries become **more skilled** and this expertise can be useful when they return to work in Britain.

Economic reasons
- Aid helps countries develop their economies. If these countries become **richer** they will be able to buy more of the manufactured goods which Britain sells abroad.
- If Britain gives bilateral aid, the developing country might **give something in return** e.g. cheaper exports of crops like coffee, tea or cotton.

Political reasons
- Britain may want **power** and influence in certain parts of the world and it will give aid to these countries. For example, a country's location may be strategically important in a larger context like a re-fuelling stop in a war situation.
- Britain is also more likely to give aid to **democracies**.

Factors countries take into account before they give aid

Figure 4.6 What questions does a country ask before giving aid?

Social	Economic	Political
'Do they need it?'	**'What's in it for me?'**	**'Are they friendly?'**
Donors check birth rates, death rates, infant mortality, life expectancy, literacy and GNI and give aid to the countries that need it most.	Donor countries will check what they get in return, like 'tied' aid spent in their countries or access to natural resources like oil.	Donor countries mostly give aid to friendly countries with a democratic government that has a good record on human rights.
'Have we got it?'	**'Will it help them?'**	**'Are they honest?'**
Donor countries check if they have the skills and expertise needed and if they can afford to give aid.	Donor countries will check to see if the aid will help develop the economy of the country receiving it.	Donor countries also check that the aid is going to the people who need it and not into the pockets of corrupt government officials.

Chapter 4

Questions and Answers

GENERAL

Give **two** reasons why European countries benefit from giving aid to African countries.

(Knowledge and Understanding, 4 marks)

To answer this question fully you must make sure that you use **PEE**. Below is a list of points you may want to include in your answer:

- tied aid
- allies.

CREDIT

Describe, in detail, some of the political factors which are considered by economically more developed countries before deciding which African countries should be given aid.

(Knowledge and Understanding, 4 marks)

To answer this question fully you must make sure that you **PEEL** the question. Below is a list of points you may want to include in your answer:

- power and influence over recipient countries
- style of government.

Hints and Tips

You may find that the wording in some of the questions in the examination paper is not the same as the headings of your notes. Don't panic! You can use the information you have, and adapt it to suit the wording of the question you are answering.

For example, if you are asked a question about **how developed countries benefit from giving aid**, simply adapt the information about **why countries give aid**. After all, when you think about it, countries give aid because they benefit from it!

Chapter 4

Does aid meet the needs of developing countries?

Sometimes there are problems with the type of aid given and it does not meet the needs of the countries receiving it. Some of the problems of different types of aid are shown in the table below.

Bilateral aid	Multilateral aid	Voluntary aid
◆ Tied to particular countries and projects that do not always meet the needs of the local people.	◆ Sometimes governments use aid for their own purposes and it does not reach the people.	◆ Rely on donations from the public, so the flow of money cannot always be guaranteed.
◆ Loans can cause problems when countries cannot repay debt.	◆ Usually a loan that has to be paid back with interest.	◆ The projects are small scale.

Sometimes a type of aid does not meet the needs of all the people receiving it. Some of the good points and bad points about the different forms of aid are shown below.

Emergency aid	Development aid	Military aid
This is short-term aid given in times of disaster. It meets basic needs at the time of the crisis but can create dependency.	This is aid given for the long-term development of the economy. It is one of the main causes of debt. Some projects do not meet basic needs and it is open to corruption.	This is aid to buy weapons and equipment. It can keep dictators in power. It can also prolong civil wars and basic needs are difficult to meet in times of conflict.

Questions and Answers

CREDIT

Explain, **in detail**, why some African countries feel that the aid they have been given is inappropriate.

(Knowledge and Understanding, 4 marks)

To answer this question fully you must make sure that you use **PEEL**. Below is a list of points you may want to include in your answer:

◆ what the aid is given for
◆ how the aid is given.

SYLLABUS AREA 4 – INTERNATIONAL RELATIONS

107

Chapter 4

Hints and Tips

Sometimes you can be given a cartoon as part of a question. When this happens you can use **TICK** to help you. TICK works like this:

Text	=	What is written on the cartoon?
Image	=	What information is in the drawing/picture?
Context	=	What topic/part of your notes is the cartoon about?
Knowledge	=	What information from your notes can you use to help you explain what the cartoon is about?

Text
Aid has not benefitted the ordinary people of this country. Government has become powerful because it has used the aid to buy arms for the army.

Image
Army has modern weapons but people have only a basic plough. People look under-nourished but still have to do heavy manual work.
Aid could have been spent on agricultural equipment to improve food production.

Image
Aid spent on tanks for the army – tanks are drving over farmland, destroying crops.
This gives the impression that government and aid donors do not care about the needs of the people.

Image
Land looks dry with no vegetation – not good for growing crops.
Aid could have been used to improve the land by irrigation, fertilisers, etc.

Context
'Does aid meet the needs of developing countries?'

Knowledge
Sometimes bilateral 'tied' aid is not used to help the ordinary people. Military aid can be used to keep governments in power.

Chapter 4

Hints and Tips

Congratulations! You have completed a syllabus area and it is time to organise your notes about the Politics of Aid and add them to your information about Alliances. Try to see how the whole syllabus area of International Relations fits together. Make sure you understand the concepts of **need** and **power** and that you know where they apply in each topic.

If you have worked through Chapters 1–4 you have also completed the KU part of your revision. Well done! Read over your notes so that you have them clear in your mind and you are ready to apply your KU information to help you with the Enquiry Skills section.

SYLLABUS AREA 4 – INTERNATIONAL RELATIONS

Chapter 5

ENQUIRY SKILLS (ES)

Enquiry Skills (ES) are a very important part of the Modern Studies course. As you already know they account for **60%** of your final grade. However, that **doesn't** mean KU is less important!

The good thing about ES questions is that they are based on techniques that you can learn and perfect. So **don't panic** when you see a long ES question in the examination – just settle down and use the techniques you have practised to answer it one step at a time!

There are two types of ES question:

Source based questions – to answer these questions you must use **all** of the sources as fully as you can.

Non-source based investigation questions – to answer these questions you must use your own knowledge as well as applying a technique.

ES questions appear in all three examinations – General, Credit and Foundation – and in all the syllabus areas.

In the next few pages we explain how to approach each type of ES question, using Syllabus Area 1 – Living in a Democracy as an example. It's a good idea to have revised the topics of Politics, Pressure Groups and Trade Unions before you start this chapter.

Source Based Questions

General
In the General paper you will be asked to answer various types of source based questions. These include:

- exaggeration
- support and oppose/for and against/agree and disagree; in some cases you may be asked to support *or* oppose – you might not always be asked to do both.
- differences
- conclusion
- option choice.

Chapter 5

In the course of a General paper you will also be required to answer a **non-source based** question. **This may appear in any of the four syllabus areas**.

> **Remember**
>
> All General questions are worth 4 marks. This means you must make at least **two points** and **give evidence**.

Exaggeration

Study Sources 1 and 2 below, then answer the question which follows.

Source 1

Greenpeace is a powerful pressure group.

Some of Greenpeace's income comes in the form of donations from supporters. Total income for Greenpeace is about £6 million per year.

Greenpeace tries to use powerful and legal methods of protest. However, on occasions some members have felt the need to break the law to draw attention to important issues. Greenpeace also lobbies MPs to try and change government policy.

Source 2

Shelter Scotland only uses peaceful campaign methods. Its members would never break the law to get things changed. They lobby MPs and use other legal methods.

Some of Shelter Scotland's income comes from donations from supporters and some from government grants. The total income of the organisation is about £2 million per year.

Shelter Scotland is an important pressure group.

> 'All pressure groups are the same.'

View of Gina Curtis

Using Sources 1 and 2 above, give **two** reasons why Gina Curtis could be accused of **exaggeration**.
Your answer must be based entirely on the sources above.

(Enquiry Skills, 4 marks)

Chapter 5

Step 1 To answer this question fully, make sure you understand that in Modern Studies 'exaggeration' means 'lie'. It is **vital** that you read all sources and the view carefully.

Remember

The sources may contain statistics, written text, graphs or cartoons. Don't be thrown – the technique you use is the same!

Step 2 Go through each source carefully and highlight the evidence that shows exaggeration. For example, you could underline it, or put a cross (X) next to it.

Step 3 Write your answer. First, quote the exaggeration, say why it is exaggerated and then give evidence from the sources to prove your point. Remember: do this twice for full marks!

Remember

It is not enough to write a list – you must **write in detail**! Also, make sure that you start a **new paragraph** for **each new point**.

Below is an answer containing the main points.

Gina Curtis is exaggerating when she says: 'All pressure groups are the same.' The sources clearly show that in terms of income Greenpeace and Shelter are very different. Source 1 shows that Greenpeace has an income of about £6 million per year, whereas, according to Source 2, Shelter has an annual income of about £2 million per year. This is a massive difference of £4 million.

Gina Curtis again exaggerates when she states that all pressure groups are the same. The sources clearly show that these two pressure groups use very different methods of campaigning. For example, in Source 1 Greenpeace is shown as occasionally breaking the law to draw attention to important issues. On the other hand, Shelter clearly states in Source 2 that it would never break the law.

Support

Study Sources 1 and 2 below, then answer the question which follows.

Source 1

Typical Council Tax, 2001/2	
City of Edinburgh	£960
City of Glasgow	£1120
Scottish Borders	£785
Western Isles	£350

Source 2

> **Extract from Radio News Broadcast**
> Council tax bills in Scotland increased by as much as 10% between 2000 and 2001. Council leaders have blamed the Scottish Executive for not giving them enough money to run services. However, some councils say that they will be able to increase spending on education and social work.

Services provided by some councils will improve next year. People in city areas will pay much more council tax than people in other areas.

View of Norman Anderson

Using **only** Sources 1 and 2, give **two** reasons to support the view of Norman Anderson.
You must use only information from the Sources above.

(Enquiry Skills, 4 marks)

In some cases this may be an 'oppose' question. Remember that the steps are the same.

Step 1 To answer this question fully, you must make sure that you give clear evidence to support the view.

Chapter 5

Step 2 Read each sentence of the view carefully. Check the source to find evidence that supports the view.

Hints and Tips

Use **HINT** to check the heading (Typical Council Tax 2001/2) of the table, the information (amount of Council Tax paid in Glasgow, Edinburgh, Borders and Western Isles), the number (amount of Council Tax paid in year 2001/2 given in £) and trend (city areas like Glasgow and Edinburgh charge more Council Tax than more rural areas like Borders and Western Isles).

It might make it easier to answer the question if you highlight the part of the source that supports the view. You could circle it, underline it or put a tick next to it.

Step 3 Start writing your answer. Write down the part of the view that can be supported and then use the evidence from the source to back this up.

It is not enough to write a list – you must write **in detail**! Also, make sure that you start a new paragraph for each new point.

Below is an answer containing the main points.

One reason to support the view of Norman Anderson is that he states: 'Services provided by some councils will improve next year.' This is clearly shown in Source 2 because we can see that spending is set to increase in social work and education.

Another reason to support the view of Norman Anderson is that he states: 'People in city areas will pay much more Council Tax than people in other areas.' This is clearly true because in Source 1 we can see that Council Tax is much more expensive in the two city areas than in the other two areas given. For example, in Glasgow Council Tax is £1,120 per year, whereas in the Western Isles it is only £350 per year. This is a massive difference of £770 per year.

Chapter 5

Differences

Study Sources 1 and 2 below, then answer the question which follows.

Source 1

Women in UNISON

UNISON is an example of a Trade Union in which women are well-represented. 72% of the membership of UNISON is female, and the proportion has been increasing quickly over recent years.

The role of Trade Unions has changed over recent years. UNISON is concerned about issues such as education, child-care, racism and sexual harassment. More women are becoming involved in union activities and taking on positions as Union officials.

Source 2

Women and the TGWU

The TGWU is one of the largest Unions in the country. 26% of its members are female – which is a big increase compared to a few years ago. Despite increasing numbers of female members, not many women have become Union officials.

Issues such as education, child-care, sexual harassment and racism are important for the TGWU. These used to be less important, but the work of Trade Unions has changed as time passed.

Sources 1 and 2 give different views about the representation of women in trade unions.
Write down **two** of the differences between these views.
You must use only information from the Sources above.

(Enquiry Skills, 4 marks)

Step 1 Read all sources carefully and think about the differences between them. To answer this question fully you must give **evidence** to clearly support the differences.

Step 2 When you are spotting the differences, make sure that they are on the same issue. Don't just randomly write down any difference!

Step 3 Start writing your answer.

It is not enough to write a list – you must write **in detail**! Also, make sure that you start a **new paragraph** for **each new point**.

ENQUIRY SKILLS (ES)

Chapter 5

Below is an answer containing the main points.

One difference in the representation of women is that in Source 1 we can see that UNISON has a very high female membership but in Source 2 we can see that this is not true for the TGWU. For example, 72% of UNISON's membership is female but only 26% of the TGWU's membership is female. This is a massive difference of 46%.

Another difference in the representation of women is that in Source 1 we can see that in UNISON many women become officials. However, Source 2 shows that the opposite is true for the TGWU. For example, Source 1 states that: 'More women are becoming involved in union activities and taking on positions as Union officials.' However, in Source 2 it states that '… not many women have become Union officials.'

Conclusion

Study the information below, then answer the question which follows.

Support for Selected Political Parties in Opinion Polls			
	Conservative	Labour	Liberal Democrat
2000	34%	44%	17%
2001	30%	46%	17%
2002	32%	41%	21%

Write down **two** conclusions about support for political parties in the Opinion Polls shown.
You must only use the information above.

(Enquiry Skills, 4 marks)

Step 1 To answer this question fully, make sure you state your **conclusion clearly**. A conclusion is a statement that shows a pattern or a general overview of the information in a source(s). State the conclusion you have reached and then start a new sentence to explain why you reached that conclusion.

Hints and Tips

Remember, use **HINT** to help get as much information as possible from the table. For example, **headings** tell you the table gives **information** about the support in the opinion polls for Labour, Conservative and Liberal Democrats in 2000, 2001 and 2002. **Number** tells you the support is given as a percentage and if you look at the **trend** you find out how support has varied for the three parties between 2000 and 2002.

Step 2 Explain why your conclusion is true.

Step 3 Provide evidence from the source to back up your conclusion.

It is not enough to write a list – you must write **in detail**! Also, make sure that you take a **new paragraph** for **each new point**. This question is worth 4 marks. Therefore you need to make two well-supported points.

Below is an answer containing the main points.

One conclusion that can be reached is that Labour had the highest support for all three years – 2000, 2001 and 2002. It is clear from the source that Labour had a higher level of support than either the Conservatives or the Liberal Democrats. For example, Labour had a support of 41% in the opinion polls in 2002, which was almost double the support for Liberal Democrats at 21%. This is a massive difference of 20%.

Another conclusion that can be drawn is that Labour has shown the biggest drop in support. For example, Conservative support dropped by 4% between 2000 and 2001 and then increased by 2% between 2001 and 2002, while Liberal Democrat support increased by 4%. In the same period, Labour support increased by 2% and then fell by 5%. This is the largest fall in support of all the three parties.

Chapter 5

Option choice question

Study Sources 1 and 2 below, then answer the question which follows.

Source 1

Information about Glenmarsh Textile Factory
Glenmarsh textile factory has lost orders from all over the world. The management wants to cut hours and pay, and to introduce retraining schemes for the workers. The Shop Steward will also have to discuss safety concerns after an accident at the factory and a complaint by two female workers that they have been treated unfairly.

Source 2

Sheila Cameron
Sheila is 55 years old and has worked at Glenmarsh for 12 years. In 1999, she completed a Health and Safety course at union headquarters. She wants to protect the jobs and pay of the workers. In previous disputes she has been a good negotiator. She is very popular with the workers.

Davie Paterson
Davie Paterson is regarded as an expert in dealing with sex discrimination cases. He also has experience of retraining schemes and spoke to the TUC conference about ways to introduce these to companies. He is 54 years old and has worked at Glenmarsh for 10 years.

Using only the information in Sources 1 and 2 above, **explain which person would be the better choice as the Shop Steward** for the workers at Glenmarsh Textiles.
Give **two** reasons for your choice.
You **must** link the information in Source 1 to the person you have chosen.

(Enquiry Skills, 4 marks)

Step 1 To answer this question fully, make sure that you **state your choice clearly**. It does not matter what choice you make, as long as you **provide evidence** to support it. It is **vital** that you read all the sources and background information in detail.

Step 2 **Link** your choice to the **background information** you have been given. At the same time, state why this makes your choice better than the other option.

Step 3 Write your answer.

It is not enough to write a list – you must write **in detail**! Also, make sure that you start a **new paragraph** for **each new point**. This question is worth **8 marks**. Therefore you need to make three or four well-supported points.

Below is an answer containing the main points.

I would choose Davie Paterson.

One reason why I chose Davie is that Source 2 states that he '… is regarded as an expert in dealing with sex discrimination cases.' This proves that he would be good at representing men and women in the workplace. This is important because in Source 1 it states that two female workers have been treated unfairly and need representation.

Another reason why I chose Davie is that Source 2 states that: 'He also has experience of retraining schemes and spoke to the TUC Conference about ways to introduce these to companies.' This proves that he would be good because workers would feel that they could talk to someone with experience of retraining. This is important because in Source 1 it states that the management want to introduce retraining schemes for workers to combat lost orders.

Credit

In the Credit paper you will be asked to answer various types of source based questions. These include:

- selective in the use of facts
- support and oppose/for and against
- conclusion
- decision making activity/option choice.

In the course of a Credit paper you will also be required to answer a **non-source based** question. **This can appear in any of the four syllabus areas.**

Chapter 5

Selective in the use of facts

Study Sources 1, 2 and 3 below and opposite, then answer the question which follows.

Source 1

What should happen to Scotland after the 2007 Scottish Parliament Election

Views of Main Parties

LIBERAL DEMOCRATS	LABOUR	CONSERVATIVE	SNP	GREENS
Increased powers for the Scottish Parliament but 'no' to independence	Scotland to remain in the United Kingdom	Scotland remains in the UK but willing to debate issues about devolved powers	Scotland to become independent after a referendum	Scotland to become an independent country

Seats in Scottish Parliament 2003 and 2007

2003: SNP 27, Labour 50 (Government), Lib Dems 17, Conservative 18, Others 10, Greens 7

2007: SNP 47 (Government), Labour 46, Lib Dems 16, Conservative 17, Others 1, Greens 2

There are 129 MSPs

Source 2

Scottish Parliament Elections (2003 and 2007)
Regional Turnout

Region	Turnout 2003	Turnout 2007
1 Central Scotland	48.5%	50.5%
2 Glasgow	41.5%	41.6%
3 Highlands and Islands	52.3%	54.7%
4 Lothians	50.5%	54.0%
5 Mid-Scotland and Fife	49.7%	52.8%
6 North East Scotland	48.3%	50.7%
7 South of Scotland	52.3%	53.6%
8 West of Scotland	53.3%	56.5%
Scotland (Total)	**49.4%**	**51.7%**

Source 3

National Identity and the Scottish Parliament
People have different views on what makes a Scot. Is it supporting our football and rugby teams; is it a willingness to wear a kilt; is it a liking for traditional Scottish music or shortbread or the consumption of our national drink?

What makes a Scot?
A person's accent appears to be a very important when people are deciding if somebody is Scottish or not. A recent survey showed that 70% of Scottish people felt that a non-white person with a Scottish accent was Scottish whilst 54% believed that a person with an English accent living in Scotland was not Scottish.

In 1999, prior to the opening of the Scottish Parliament, research carried out for the Government showed 25% of people in Scotland felt 'Scottish not British' and 11% said they would describe themselves as 'British not Scottish'. SNP voters and young people were much more likely to say they were Scottish whilst the elderly and Conservative voters were more likely to say they were 'British'. When the research was repeated in 2006, 32% of Scottish people said they would describe themselves as 'Scottish not British' and only 9% of those asked said that they were 'British not Scottish'.

The West of Scotland Region had the largest increase in voter turnout. In 2007, there were more MSPs in favour of independence than ever before and, since the opening of the Scottish Parliament, people feel more Scottish.

View of Callum Wishart

Using **only** Sources 1, 2 and 3, explain **the extent to which** Callum Wishart could be accused of being **selective in the use of facts**.

(Enquiry Skills, 8 marks)

Chapter 5

Step 1 To answer this question fully, make sure that you understand that 'selective in the use of facts' means that you must spot **both truth and lies**. You must also state the **extent** to which the person is being selective. In some cases there may only be a few elements of truth or lies. It is **vital** that you read all sources and the view thoroughly. Remember: sources may contain statistics, written text, graphs and cartoons. Don't be thrown – the technique is always the same!

Step 2 At Credit level, organising the information is very important to gaining a good mark. Go through each source and highlight what is true and what is a lie. You could circle one and underline another, use different coloured highlighters or tick (✓) where you find truth and cross (X) where you find a lie. You must make an explicit link between the view and the sources.

Step 3 Provide source evidence to back up your answer **and** state the extent to which the person has been selective. This can be done by drawing either one overall conclusion or multiple mini conclusions as to the extent of selectivity on each part of the view. Have they been 'very selective' (more lies than truths), 'a little bit selective' (more truths than lies) or 'not selective at all' (equal balance of truths and lies)? The degree of selectivity varies.

It is not enough to write a list – you must write **in detail**! Also make sure that you start a **new paragraph** for **each new point**. This question is worth **8 marks**. Therefore you need to make four well-supported points.

Below is an answer containing the main points.

Source 2 shows that Callum Wishart is selective in the use of facts when he says 'The West of Scotland had the largest increase in voter turnout'. The source shows that although the turnout increased in the West of Scotland by 3.2%, the turnout in Lothians increased by 3.5%. Therefore, Callum is incorrect because Lothians had the largest increase in voter turnout.

Source 1 shows that Callum is telling the truth and therefore is not selective in the use of facts when he states 'In 2007, there were more MSPs in favour of independence than ever before'. The source shows that the SNP and Green party are in favour of independence. Their overall share of seats in the Scottish Parliament has increased from 34 MSPs in 2003 to 49 MSPs by 2007. Therefore, Callum is correct in his view.

Source 3 also shows that Callum is not selective in the use of facts when he says 'since the opening of the Scottish Parliament, people feel more Scottish'. A quarter (25%) felt more Scottish than British in 1999. This increased to nearly a third (32%) in 2006. Therefore Callum is telling the truth.

Overall, Callum was slightly selective in his use of facts because two of his statements are correct and only one is wrong.

Chapter 5

Support and oppose/for and against

Study the information below, then answer the question which follows.

Proportion of workers who are trade union members (Great Britain 1990–2000)

	1990	1995	2000
Number of union members (thousands)	8835	7309	7321
All employment	33.9%	28.8%	27%
Gender			
Male	44%	35%	30%
Female	32%	30%	29%
Type of work			
Manual	42%	33%	28%
Non-manual	35%	32%	30%
Full- or part-time work			
Full-time	43%	36%	33%
Part-time	22%	21%	23%
Employment Sector			
Manufacturing	44%	34%	28%
Services	37%	33%	31%

> Trade unions have become more gender equal since 1990. Unions are now strongest in manual work and the manufacturing sector despite recent changes in British industry.

View of Frances Naismith

Using **only** the information above, give **one** reason to **support** and **one** reason to **oppose** the view of Frances Naismith.

(Enquiry Skills, 4 marks)

Step 1 To answer this question fully, make sure that you can understand that support means 'for' and oppose means 'against'. It is **vital** that you read all sources and the view thoroughly.

Hints and Tips

The **trend** is particularly important in this source, so make sure you use **HINT**. Look back at the information on 'Changes in trade union membership' in Chapter 1 to remind yourself about how to deal with this kind of table.

Step 2 When you are given a view, read each sentence carefully, and use the information in the source to find evidence to prove whether or not that part of the view can be supported or opposed.

Go through the view and highlight the part of the view which can be supported by the sources and which part can be opposed. You could circle one and underline another, use different coloured highlighters or tick (✓) the part that can be supported and cross (X) the part that can be opposed.

It doesn't matter which code you use, as long as you find a technique that allows you to **organise** your information **quickly** under examination conditions.

Step 3 Start writing your answer. You must clearly highlight which part of the view can be supported by the evidence in the sources and which can be opposed. The evidence used must be explicitly linked to the view.

It is not enough to write a list – you must write **in detail**! Also, make sure that you start a **new paragraph** for **each new point**. This question is worth **4 marks**. Therefore you need to make two well-supported points.

Below is an answer containing the main points.

One reason to support the view of Frances Naismith is because he states that: 'Trade unions have become more gender equal since 1990.' This is clearly shown in the source where we can see that between 1990 and 2000 the difference between the proportion of male and female trade union members has reduced to the point that they are almost the same. For example, in 1990 there was a relatively large difference of 12%, in favour of men. However, by 2000 this margin had reduced to 1%, with men at 30% and women at 29%.

One reason to oppose the view of Frances Naismith is because he states: 'Unions are now strongest in manual work…' This is untrue because in the source we can see that a higher proportion of non-manual workers are now union members. This changed in the year 2000. In 2000, for example, 28% of manual workers were trade union members compared with 30% of non-manual. This is a difference of 2%.

Conclusion

Study the cartoon below, then answer the question which follows.

Using **only** the cartoon above, what **conclusions** can be reached about the attitudes of people towards elections?

You must reach **two** separate conclusions.

(Enquiry Skills, 4 marks)

Step 1 To answer this question fully, make sure that you **state your conclusion clearly**. A conclusion is a statement that shows a pattern or a general overview of the information in a source(s).

State the conclusion you have reached and then start a new sentence to explain why you reached that conclusion.

Hints and Tips

The source in this question is a cartoon – use **TICK** to help. The **text** tells you about the attitudes towards elections and voting. The **image** shows you various age groups and their level of interest in elections. The **context** is therefore using your right to vote and voter apathy, so think about what **background knowledge** you can use to help you come to a conclusion *quickly*!

If you need more help with how TICK works, look back at the Politics of Aid topic in Chapter 4.

Step 2 At this stage you should explain why your conclusion is true.

Step 3 Now provide evidence from the sources to back up your conclusion. You may gain better marks if you make comparisons in, and between, sources.

It is not enough to write a list – you must write **in detail**! Also make sure that you start a **new paragraph** for **each new point**. This question is worth **4 marks**. Therefore you need to make two well-supported points.

Below is an answer containing the main points.

One conclusion that can be reached is that the older generation is far more likely to vote than the younger generation. It is clear to see from the source that the elderly woman is the only member of the family interested in voting. The rest of the family seem disinterested. For example, we can clearly see that the elderly woman says: 'I need a lift to the polling station', whereas the young woman is more interested in going to the pub.

Another conclusion that can be drawn is that electoral turnout is decreasing. From the source it is clear that this family reflect this. The television programme reinforces this further. For example, the television programme states 'Turnout Down' and only one person, out of four who are eligible to vote, is actually interested in doing so.

Decision Making Activity/Option Choice

Study the Background Information about Gleninch and Sources 1 and 2, then answer the question which follows.

Background information about Gleninch Constituency

- Gleninch is a constituency in the north of Scotland with a population of 35,265 people. It is a largely rural area with only one town, Inverinch, and a large number of scattered villages. The traditional industries of farming and fishing have been in decline in recent years. The unemployment rate is well above the national average.
- Many young people leave the area, moving to the big cities throughout the UK to look for jobs or to attend college or university.
- Tourism is very important to the local economy, with a lot of people employed in hotels, bed and breakfast accommodation and restaurants. Tourists tend to visit the area for a few days on short breaks, attracted by rare wildlife and spectacular, unspoilt scenery. However, there are a number of transport problems in the constituency, including high petrol prices and poor public transport.
- There is a proposal to build a wind farm in the area. This would involve the construction of 6 large wind turbines along the coast, as well as a 15 mile long power line built on tall pylons to take electricity to the rest of the country. This would create a few temporary construction jobs but will disturb local wildlife and impact on the scenery of the area.
- An American mining company wants to build a huge 'super-quarry' into a mountainside near Gleninch. This will produce crushed rock to build roads, railways and houses throughout the UK. The new quarry will create 150 new jobs in Gleninch.
- At the last General Election, the constituency was won by the Labour Party with a majority of just over 1000 votes. The Liberal Democrats came second. They are convinced that, with the right candidate, they can win the seat at the next election.

A Statistical Profile of Gleninch Constituency (2006)

	Gleninch	Comparison with Scottish Average
Average Income	£21,185	–14%
Income Support claimants	15.1%	+22%
Unemployment Rate	5.6%	+13%
School leavers with no qualifications	3.6%	–33%
School leavers with Highers	58.6%	+13%
Serious Assaults	8.8 (per 10,000 people)	–73%
Housebreaking	3.8 (per 10,000 people)	–93%
Road Accidents	57 casualties	–44%

Survey of Local Liberal Democrat Members

Question: *How important are these issues to people in the area?*

Issue	Unimportant	Not very important	Fairly important	Very important
Environment	5%	25%	40%	30%
Health	2%	10%	53%	35%
Jobs	0%	0%	48%	52%
Women in Parliament	15%	52%	22%	11%

There are two people hoping to be selected by the Liberal Democratic Party to be the Party's candidate at the next General Election. Here are extracts from speeches they have made.

Source 1

Extract from campaign speech by Kirsty Reid

- I support the proposed wind farm as it will provide many local jobs and help the local environment.
- Our local schools provide an excellent education. If selected, I will work to ensure this continues.
- Women make up over half the country's population and yet there are still very few of us who are MPs. This is a major priority for local party members and is an important reason why I should be the candidate.
- The local economy has been in decline recently. We need more jobs to keep our young people in the area. The new quarry will help with this, and I will work hard to see that it is allowed to go ahead.
- To attract more people to the area we need to improve transport links. I will make this a priority.

Source 2

> **Extract from campaign speech by Robbie McKay**
> - Tourism is very important to the area and so I will oppose the new wind farm as it will be an ugly blot on the landscape and deter tourists.
> - Crime in Gleninch is among the worst in Scotland. I will campaign to improve policing in the area.
> - Although new jobs are important, local Liberal Democrats are much more concerned about the environment. The new quarry will put more heavy lorries on our roads which are already more dangerous than the rest of the country. I will oppose it going ahead.
> - The issue of health will be one of my main concerns, just as it is for local party members.
> - Compared to the rest of the country, the people of Gleninch are not well-off. I will do all I can to improve this.

Use **only** the information about Gleninch and Sources 1 and 2 above:

(i) State **which person** would be the **more suitable** to be selected by the Liberal Democratic Party as their candidate for this constituency at the next General Election.

(ii) Give **three detailed reasons to support your choice**.

(iii) Give **two detailed** reasons why you **rejected** the other candidate.

In your answer, you **must relate** information about the constituency to the information about the **two** candidates.

(Enquiry Skills, 10 marks)

Step 1 To answer this question fully, make sure that you **state your choice clearly**. It does not matter what choice you make, as long as you **provide evidence** to support it, and state why the other option is not as good. It is **vital** that you read all the sources and background information thoroughly. Remember: sources may contain written text, statistics, graphs and charts (use HINT) or cartoons (use TICK).

Step 2 When you begin to write your answer you must **link** your choice to the **background information** you have been given.

Step 3 You have completed the main part of the question. Now you have to give a reason for rejecting/not choosing the other option. Remember: you can't repeat a point you've already used – it's got to be fresh.

It is not enough to write a list – you must write **in detail**! Also make sure that you start a **new paragraph** for **each new point**. This question is worth **10 marks**. Therefore you need to make five well-supported points.

Below is an answer containing the main points.

(i)

I would choose **Kirsty Reid**.

(ii)

One reason why I chose Kirsty Reid is that she states that she 'will work to ensure that our local schools continue to provide an excellent education'. The statistical profile of Gleninch shows that school leavers with Highers is 13% above the Scottish average and that school leavers with no qualifications is 33% below the Scottish average.

The second reason why I chose Kirsty Reid is that she supports the 'new quarry because it will provide jobs to stop the decline of the local economy'. The background information about Gleninch shows that 150 new jobs will be created in the quarry.

The third and final reason why I chose Kirsty is because she wants to 'improve transport links and make this a priority'. This is important because there are a number of transport problems in the constituency such as poor public transport and high petrol prices.

(iii)

The first reason why I rejected Robbie McKay is that he states in his campaign speech 'crime in Gleninch is the worst in Scotland. I will campaign to improve policing in the area'. The statistics clearly show that crime in the area is quite low, with housebreaking 93% lower than the Scottish average, and serious assaults 73% lower. Crime is therefore not the worst in Scotland.

Finally, I rejected Robbie because he states that 'local Liberal Democrats are much more concerned about the environment than jobs'. This is incorrect because the survey shows that just over half (52%) think that jobs are very important, compared to only under a third (30%) for the environment.

Foundation

In the Foundation paper you will be asked to answer various types of source based questions. These include:

- exaggeration
- support and oppose/for and against/agree and disagree/true and false; in some cases you may be asked to support *or* oppose – you might not always be asked to do both.
- differences
- option choice.

In the course of a Foundation paper you will also be required to answer a **non-source based question. This may come up in any of the four syllabus areas.** Remember: all Foundation questions are usually worth no more than 4 marks. This means you must make two points and give evidence.

The steps taken will be exactly the same as the General paper but you will not be expected to provide as much detail. This does not mean that you can write one-word answers. You must write in sentences and use source evidence. However, there are some questions that can be answered by ticking a box. You must make sure that you read questions fully and take time to think about your answer.

Chapter 5

Non-Source Based Investigtion Questions

General

You are investigating the topic in the box below.

> The work of a Local Councillor

Answer questions (a), (b) and (c) which follow

(a) As part of the **Planning Stage**, give **two** relevant **aims** for your investigation.

(Enquiry Skills, 2 marks)

You see the following advertisement in the local paper.

Study the advertisement carefully, then answer the question which follows.

Mary Millar, Inverdee Councillor
Answering Your Questions / Solving Your Problems

Surgeries will be held as follows:

Inverdee Town Hall
7.00–9.00 pm, first and third
Tuesday each month
(No appointment required)

Inverdee Secondary School
7.00–9.00 pm, second and fourth
Tuesday each month
(No appointment required)

Contact Mary Millar
Inverdee City Council Offices
Inverbrig Road
Inverdee

Phone: Inverdee 307086
e-mail: mmillar@inverdeecouncil.gov.uk

My door is  always open

(b) You have decided to try and contact a local councillor to help you in your investigation.
From the advertisement above, choose **two** ways in which you could contact a local councillor.
For **each** way you have chosen, explain why it is a **good** way to get information to help in your investigation.

(Enquiry Skills, 4 marks)

(c) You also decide to use copies of your local newspaper from the past two years to help with your investigation.
Give **one** advantage and **one** disadvantage of using **past copies of the local newspaper** for your investigation.

(Enquiry Skills, 2 marks)

Chapter 5

You do **not** have to take a 'steps' approach to this question. Just take the questions one at a time and answer them as accurately as possible.

(a) Below are possible aims that you can use. Remember: you should give **two** – we have given more to show you a variety of possible answers:

- *To find out what work a local councillor does to help the people who live in their ward.*
- *To find out how many surgeries a local councillor holds per month in the local area.*
- *To find out where and when local councillors hold their surgeries.*
- *To find out how many hours' work a local councillor does per week.*

(b) Remember to read the question carefully. This question asks you about specific ways you can contact your councillor. You must ensure that you highlight why these methods are positive.

One method you could use to contact your local councillor is to attend their surgery. In this case you could attend Inverdee Town Hall or the Secondary School. This method is good because it allows you to meet with the councillor face to face. Often people are more comfortable dealing with people this way rather than over the telephone. As a result, they will find it much easier to pick up on the information they are given.

Another method you could use to contact your local councillor is to use email. In this case you email Mary Millar at mmillar@inverdeecouncil.gov.uk. This method is good because it allows you to contact your local councillor with ease and it is both quick and inexpensive. Email is a good way to gather information because you can take your time composing the message and ensure that you include all the required detail. It also gives you the ability to keep in regular contact with your councillor.

(c)

One advantage of using past copies of local newspapers is that they are readily available from both the local library and the newspaper office. This means that you can access the information quite quickly.

One disadvantage of using past copies of local newspapers is that they are out of date, and as a result may contain totally irrelevant information. For example, Mary Millar may not have been a councillor two years ago.

Chapter 5

Credit

In the Credit Modern Studies paper you will be asked to complete a **hypothesis** question. This is the non-source based Enquiry Skills question in your paper. This is worth a great deal – in the case of Credit it's worth **10 marks**. In the same way as you have with the source based Enquiry Skills questions, you will be able to perfect the skill with practice.

Hypothesis questions are easy to recognise because they have a distinctive logo beside them. It's a head with a question mark in it.

Put simply, a **hypothesis** is a statement that you **must** be able to prove or disprove. It must be **relevant** to the investigation topic.

The investigation topic is located at the top of the page in a box.

To be able to prove or disprove your hypothesis you must give two relevant aims.

Remember

This can't be a repeat of the hypothesis itself. You should always start your aims with:

To find out…   if
                 what
                 when
                 where
                 why
                 how

Now that you have done the difficult bit, all you have to do is apply the knowledge you have about different methods of enquiry. Methods of enquiry are simply the ways people find information. It could be from a library, a CD-ROM, the Internet, etc. You must be able to describe at least two advantages and two disadvantages of each method.

ENQUIRY SKILLS (ES)

Chapter 5

Advantages and disadvantages of enquiry methods

Make sure that you can explain **two** arguments **for** and **against** each method.

Method	Advantages	Disadvantages
Databases	◆ A lot of information ◆ You can print out the information	◆ You will probably need a PC to use the information ◆ Analysing the information will be time-consuming
Internet	◆ Quick to access ◆ Information is updated regularly	◆ You need a PC with a modem ◆ It can offer too much information, which can be time-consuming
Questionnaire	◆ Quite cheap ◆ Easy to get people to answer	◆ For it to be valid you need a lot of responses ◆ People may not tell the truth
Attitude Survey – requires opinions	◆ People have the chance to express their opinions ◆ Good for conscience issues where people feel strongly, like abortion or animal rights	◆ Needs care when making up ◆ More difficult to analyse responses
Interview	◆ Allows detailed questions ◆ Interview can be extended if it is going well	◆ The person being interviewed may not respond well to the questions ◆ Answers may be too personal
Letter	◆ Simple and cheap to make up and send ◆ Quick	◆ Questions need to be kept simple ◆ Not everyone replies
Observation/fieldwork	◆ You can observe real behaviour ◆ You can choose a time and place for observation	◆ People may change their behaviour because you are there ◆ People may not like being observed
Library research	◆ Huge amount of material available ◆ Access is free	◆ There can be too much material ◆ The library is not always open when you need access to it
Use of the media	◆ Cheap and accessible ◆ TV and newspapers are up to date	◆ Newspapers are biased ◆ TV news items can be very short, giving little analysis

How to approach hypothesis questions: example 1

When you are given the investigation topic, it is useful to break it down into subtopics. Here is an example of an investigation topic.

> Health Care in the United States

Aspects related to health care in the US include: Life expectancy, Health insurance, Obesity, Cancer rates, Cost of health care, Blue Shield and Blue Cross, etc.

Once you have your subtopics, you are now in a position to state a hypothesis using 'G-RAT'. This acronym is short for:

- gender
- race
- age
- time.

A hypothesis is merely a statement that can be proved true or false. Try to reach a hypothesis which includes one of the four variables listed above using one of your subtopics. This then allows a comparison to be made. For example:

- Women are more likely to have health insurance than men.
- Hispanics are less likely to have health insurance than APIs.
- Elderly people are less likely to have health insurance than those aged 18–24.
- More Americans have health insurance now in 2009 than in 2000.

Once you have stated your hypothesis, you then have to reach two relevant aims. Use any of the other three variables above from 'G-RAT' to help. For example, if your hypothesis was 'Women are more likely to have health insurance than men', then your aims could be:

- I aim to find out if African American women have higher rates of health insurance than African American men.
- I aim to find out if more younger women have private health insurance than younger men.
- I aim to find out whether women have always had greater rates of health insurance than men'.

To recap:

1. Divide the investigation topic into smaller subtopics relevant to the investigation.
2. Use 'G-RAT' to state a hypothesis.
3. Use 'G-RAT' to make relevant aims. Try using any of the variables that you have not yet used.

Chapter 5

How to approach hypothesis questions: example 2

When you are given the investigation topic, it is useful to break it down into subtopics. Here is an example of an investigation topic.

> Help for Families in the UK

Aspects related to help for families in the UK include: child benefit, New Deal for Lone Parents, Tax Credits, EMA, etc.

Once you have your subtopics, you are now in a position to state a hypothesis using 'G-RAT'. This acronym is short for:

- gender
- race
- age
- time.

A hypothesis is merely a statement that can be proved true or false. Try to reach a hypothesis which includes one of the four variables listed above using one of your subtopics. This then allows a comparison to be made. For example:

- Female headed households receive greater tax credits from the Government than male headed households.
- Minority families are less likely to claim tax credits than White families.
- More elderly pensioner households claimed tax credits than younger families.
- More lone parent families claimed tax credits in 2009 than in 2008.

Once you have stated your hypothesis, you then have to reach two relevant aims. Use any of the other three variables above from 'G-RAT' to help. For example, if your hypothesis was 'Minority families are less likely to claim tax credits than White families', then your aims could be:

- I aim to find out what percentage of Indian female lone parent families are entitled to tax credits than white lone parent families.
- I aim to find out if older minority families receive more money in tax credits than younger White families.
- I aim to find out whether minority families have always claimed more tax credits than white families.

To recap:

1. Divide the investigation topic into smaller subtopics relevant to the investigation.
2. Use 'G-RAT' to state a hypothesis.
3. Use 'G-RAT' to make relevant aims. Try using any of the variables that you have not yet used.

Hypothesis question

> You have been asked to carry out an investigation on the topic below.
>
> **Investigation Topic – The methods used by pressure groups to influence MPs**

(a) State a relevant **hypothesis** for your investigation.

(Enquiry Skills, 2 marks)

(b) Give **two** aims or headings to help you prove **or** disprove your hypothesis.

(Enquiry Skills, 2 marks)

(c) You decide to visit a library to help with your investigation.
For **one** of your chosen aims or headings, describe how you would find information using a library.

(Enquiry Skills, 2 marks)

(d) You also decide to use a questionnaire.
Describe, **in detail**, **two** possible **disadvantages** of a questionnaire as a method of finding out information for this investigation.

(Enquiry Skills, 4 marks)

You do **not** have to take a 'steps' approach to this question. Just take the questions one at a time and answer them as accurately as possible.

(a) Possible hypothesis may include:

i.

Some methods used by pressure groups have been more effective in influencing MPs than others.

ii.

Pressure groups have no influence on MPs.

You may have thought of other potential hypotheses and you may want to check these with your teacher.

(b) Below are two aims for each hypothesis:

i.

To find out why some methods used by Greenpeace are more effective than others.

Chapter 5

To find out if protests have been more successful than petitions in influencing MPs in recent years.

ii.

To find out how many MPs have joined pressure groups as a result of the methods they use.

To find out what methods used by pressure groups have been most successful in influencing the decisions made by MPs.

(c) Remember to read the question carefully. This question asks you specifically about the use of the library and it also asks you to link this to one of your aims.

There are many ways in which I could use the library to research my aims. I could use the books in the library to find information on the various methods used by pressure groups in Britain to influence the Government. For example, I could use the library reference system to look up key words like 'Greenpeace' and 'pressure group methods'. It would give me a list of results from which I would select the most relevant books.

(d) Below are two disadvantages of using a questionnaire.

One disadvantage of using a questionnaire is that people may not want to fill them out because it is time-consuming. For example, if someone is a working single parent with young children they may find it very difficult to find the time to fully answer the questions they have been provided with.

Another disadvantage of using a questionnaire is that if it is carried out by post there may be very few returns. Many people are unwilling, or unable, to spend time and effort filling out and posting off their response.

Hints and Tips

Congratulations! You have completed the Enquiry Skills section.

If you have worked through the book, you will also be well prepared to tackle the KU and the ES questions in the examination.

We hope you will make good use of the knowledge, skills and techniques you have acquired and will approach your examination with confidence.

Good luck!